VOICES OF THE MARTYRS

THE TWELVE

KINGSTONE
COMICS

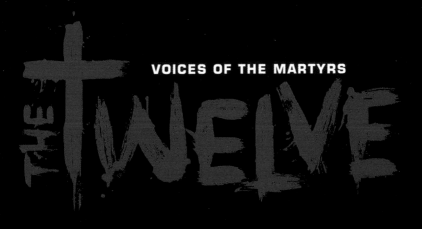

VOICES OF THE MARTYRS

THE TWELVE

WRITER:

BEN AVERY

EDITOR:

KELLY AYRIS

LETTERS:

ZACH MATHENY

PRODUCTION DESIGN:

NATE BUTLER, ZACH MATHENY, KEN RANEY

Published by Kingstone Comics
www.KingstoneMedia.com
Copyright © 2014

Printed in USA

KINGSTONE
COMICS

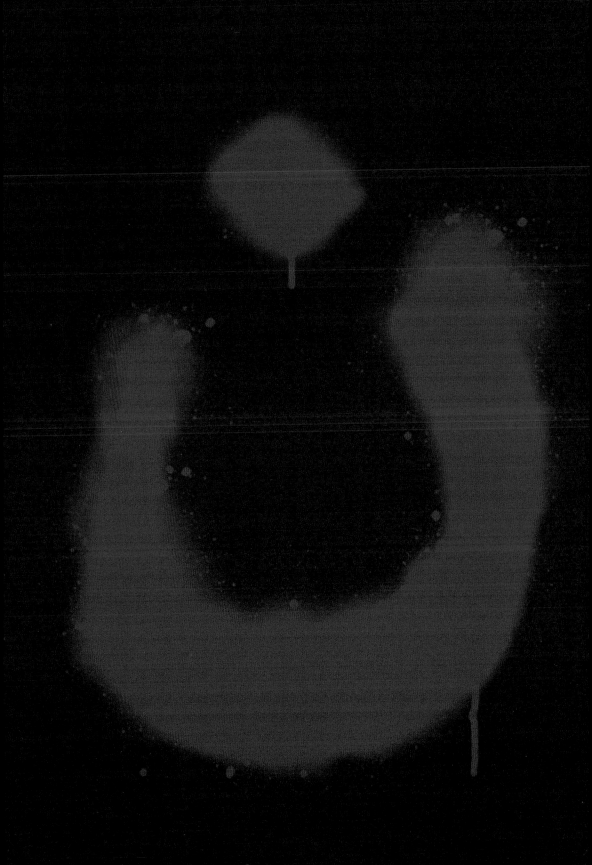

A New Symbol for Persecuted Christians

Within the first centuries following Jesus' death and resurrection, believers began to use several symbols to identify themselves as followers of Jesus Christ. One commonly used symbol was the "ichthus," from the Greek word meaning "fish."

The ichthus is thought to have been used by Christians in part as a secret symbol that wouldn't be recognized by persecutors. Today Christians are persecuted in more than 60 countries, including Muslim, communist and Hindu nations.

In Iraq, Islamic extremists are using a symbol of their own to identify Christians. In Mosul, the Islamists are using the Arabic "N" (pronounced nun) to label Christians' homes. The spray-painted "N" identifies property as belonging to "Nazarenes," or followers of Jesus of Nazareth. By marking their property, the extremists are laying claim to it.

In addition, Iraqi believers have been given an ultimatum: convert to Islam, pay an exorbitant tax, leave the area or be killed. Most Christians have chosen to flee, often with only the clothes on their backs.

We stand with our persecuted brothers and sisters, gladly identifying ourselves as "N" — followers of Jesus. We will not let them suffer alone.

Are You "N"?

If you would like to know more about what it means for our Christian brothers and sisters to live in the presence of Islamic extremists and to know how you can stand with them, please visit www.i-am-n.com.

AINA(www.aina.org)

The Voice of the Martyrs

www.persecution.com

The first followers of Jesus were called apostles. These men were sent forth by Jesus Christ and saw firsthand His miracles and resurrection. They were eyewitnesses of His majesty (2 Peter 1:16). The apostles had something else in common—all but one was martyred, or killed for his faith.

The Greek word for "martyr" (*martys*) meant "witness" in its original usage. It was most often used in the sense of "bearing witness or testimony to the truth." During the early Christian centuries, the word "martyr" was used to identify a believer who was called to witness for his religious belief and endured suffering or death because of that witness. Those who did not die because of their testimony were called "confessors," while those who died became known as "martyrs." The word "martyr" is first used in Acts 22:20 in reference to Stephen.

While the resurrection of Jesus Christ is discounted by unbelievers, the apostles serve as one of the most powerful proofs of its authenticity. One of their own requirements for the man who replaced Judas Iscariot was that he be a witness to the life, death and resurrection of Jesus Christ (Acts 1:21-26). If any of the apostles had doubted the truth of Jesus' resurrection, surely at least one of them would have avoided persecution by saying, "Stop the torture. It's a sham; it's not true." Yet all of the apostles held fast to the truth that Jesus Christ was (and is) alive and is God's son.

Were these men super saints? How are they different from us? What made them so willing to die such painful and torturous deaths? What can their lives and deaths teach us?

The apostles knew without doubt that Jesus was alive and was God's son, and they also knew that they had been called to proclaim that truth to others. God had shown them, through the person of Jesus Christ, the only way to salvation, and they were compelled to "teach all nations" His message of grace through faith in Christ.

Being martyred as Christ's witness did not end during the first century. It still happens today in more than 60 countries around the world. Though primarily occurring in regions such as Africa, the Middle East and Asia, many are paying the ultimate price because of their decision to be Christ's witness among their family and community.

The apostles made a decision that they would follow Christ—no matter the cost. But what about you and me? Is the name of Jesus on our lips? Are we courageously bearing witness to Christ's work in our own lives?

It is our prayer that the lives and deaths of the men portrayed in this graphic novel remind each of us that it's worth following Christ— whatever the cost.

ART A. AYRIS
PUBLISHER

The Stories of the 12 Apostles

1. MATTHEW
Pencils: Claude St. Aubin
Inks: Randy Emberlin
Colors: Josh Ray

63. PETER
Pencils: Agapito Delos Santos &
  Karl Comendador
Inks: Agapito Delos Santos &
  Karl Comendador
Colors: Chris Sotomayer

25. MATTHIAS
Pencils: Claude St. Aubin
Inks: Roland Paris
Colors: Tom Smith

99. JUDAS / THADDEUS
Pencils: Ariel Medel
Inks: Al Milgrom
Colors: Josh Ray

31. JOHN
Pencils: Eduardo Garcia
Inks: Charles Barnett
Colors: Andrew Crossley

103. ANDREW
Pencils: Caio Cacau
Inks: DYM
Colors: Joel Chua

45. SIMON THE ZEALOT
Pencils: Daniel Kopalek
Inks: Daniel Kopalek
Colors: Tom Smith

121. NATHANAEL / BARTHOLOMEW
Pencils: Frank Fosco
Inks: Frank Frosco
Colors: Tom Smith

49. THOMAS
Pencils: Claude St. Aubin
Inks: Jason Moore
Colors: Tom Smith

127. PHILIP
Pencils: Ariel Medel
Inks: Roland Paris
Colors: Tom Smith

59. JAMES THE LESS
Pencils: Claude St. Aubin
Inks: Jason Moore
Colors: Tom Smith

135. JAMES THE GREATER
Pencils: Ariel Medel
Inks: Al Milgrom
Colors: Tom Smith

MATTHEW
"The Tax Collector"

"AS JESUS WENT ON FROM
THERE, HE SAW A MAN NAMED
MATTHEW SITTING AT THE
TAX COLLECTOR'S BOOTH.
'FOLLOW ME,' HE TOLD HIM,
AND MATTHEW GOT UP AND
FOLLOWED HIM."
MATTHEW 9:9 (NIV)

NAME: MATTHEW,
ALSO KNOWN AS LEVI

FAMILY: ALPHAEUS, FATHER

OCCUPATION: TAX COLLECTOR
FOR THE ROMAN GOVERNMENT

GREETINGS, MATTHEW.

YES, YES.

MATTHEW, WHO, BECAUSE HE WAS JEWISH, WAS EDUCATED IN THE SCRIPTURES AND WAYS OF THE JEWS.

MATTHEW, WHO COLLECTED TAXES FROM THE JEWISH PEOPLE, BUT COLLECTED THE MONEY FOR THE ROMAN GOVERNMENT.

MATTHEW! YOU DID NOT COME TO ARION'S FEAST LAST WEEK!

I WAS NOT IN THE MOOD FOR FEASTING.

MATTHEW, WHO WAS BORN A JEW, BUT WHO SERVED ROME.

YOUR ATTENTION!

WE'VE HAD MORE COMPLAINTS THAT YOU HAVE BEEN OVERCHARGING THE PEOPLE OF CAPERNAUM FOR THEIR TAXES!

I DO NOT CARE ABOUT THOSE COMPLAINTS.

BUT YOUR COLLECTIONS HAVE BEEN LOW.

PEOPLE HAVE BEEN REFUSING TO PAY ME!

I AM AUTHORIZED TO ALLOW YOU TWENTY EXTRA SOLDIERS TO USE AS YOU SEE FIT.

IF YOU CANNOT COLLECT WHAT IS EXPECTED, BE ASSURED YOU WILL LOSE SOME, OR ALL, OF YOUR PAY FOR THE MONTH!

DO YOU MIND IF I TAKE FIVE OF THOSE SOLDIERS?

I KNOW EXACTLY WHERE I WANT TO GO FIRST.

I DO NOT THINK I WILL NEED ANY OF THEM TODAY.

OTHER THAN THE USUAL GUARDS I NEED FOR PROTECTION.

3

ROME WAS ONE OF HISTORY'S MOST POWERFUL EMPIRES.

AND THEY RULED OVER THE LAND OF THE JEWS.

THE ROMANS GAVE THE JEWISH PEOPLE FREEDOM TO WORSHIP AS THEY WANTED.

AND THEY HAD A LIMITED FREEDOM TO GOVERN THEMSELVES.

BUT ROME WAS IN CONTROL. THERE WAS NO DOUBT OF THAT.

ROME HAD THE POWER.

ROME HAD CONTROL.

HERE. TAKE IT. THIS IS ROBBERY, YOU KNOW!

THE ROADS ROME HAS BUILT WEREN'T BUILT FOR FREE, TOBIAS.

AND HOW ARE YOU ON THIS FINE DAY, MATTHEW?

PLEASE, I'M COUNTING.

OH, IT'S ALL THERE, I ASSURE YOU!

I STILL HAVE TO COUNT.

OF COURSE YOU DO!

OF COURSE YOU DO!

BEING A TAX COLLECTOR WAS AN EASIER JOB THAN SOME.

I'LL HAVE YOU KNOW, I ACTUALLY WORKED FOR THIS MONEY, YOU PILE OF DIRT --

THAT'S ENOUGH OF THAT, DIRTBALL!

EASIER THAN FISHING OR FARMING.

OR EVEN BEGGING.

I WORK TO FEED MY FAMILY, NOT THE FAMILIES OF CORRUPT POLITICIANS AND TAX COLLECTORS LIKE YOU! YOU'RE LUCKY YOU HAVE THOSE BRUTES THERE TO PROTECT YOU NOW!

IF THE ROMANS WERE HATED, THE JEWISH MEN WHO HELPED THE ROMANS WERE EVEN MORE HATED.

SO MATTHEW WAS AN UNUSUAL MAN FOR JESUS TO CHOOSE.

HAD MATTHEW BEEN THINKING ABOUT THIS JOB?

HAD HE BEEN FEELING BAD ABOUT WHAT HE WAS DOING?

WHAT'S GOING ON?

HAD MATTHEW HEARD OF JESUS BEFORE THAT DAY?

HAD MATTHEW MAYBE EVEN SPOKEN TO JESUS BEFORE THAT DAY?

OR WAS THIS THE FIRST TIME THEY EVER MET?

DID MATTHEW HEAR JESUS TEACH BEFORE THAT DAY?

IT'S QUITE POSSIBLE. THERE IS NO WAY TO KNOW.

ALL WE KNOW IS THAT MATTHEW HEARD JESUS ON THAT DAY.

AND MATTHEW RESPONDED.

HE GOT UP --

YOU'VE GOT THIS.

WHAT ARE YOU DOING?

I'M QUITTING. YOU WANT TO COME WITH ME?

TEACHER, I HAVE SO MUCH TO LEARN.

LET'S GO, MATTHEW.

AND THE FIRST THING MATTHEW DID WHEN HE CHOSE TO FOLLOW JESUS --

-- WAS TO INTRODUCE JESUS TO ALL HIS FRIENDS.

THIS WAS NOT UNUSUAL. THE OTHER DISCIPLES DID THIS, TOO.

BUT MATTHEW DID IT A BIT DIFFERENTLY.

HE HELD A FEAST FOR JESUS.

A FEAST FOR HIS FRIENDS.

AND WHO WERE THOSE FRIENDS?

OTHER TAX COLLECTORS.

FELIX WAS NOT HAPPY WHEN I TOLD HIM YOU QUIT!

THERE WILL ALWAYS BE SOMEONE WILLING TO TAKE MY PLACE.

YOU'RE A SMART ONE, GOOD WITH NUMBERS, YOU UNDERSTAND PEOPLE.

WHY ARE YOU LEAVING ALL THIS TO FOLLOW A STREET PREACHER?

BECAUSE I BELIEVE IN WHAT HE IS PREACHING!

TAKE SOME TIME TO LISTEN TO WHAT HE SAYS, MY FRIEND!

I MAY BE SMART, BUT HE IS WISE!

HE PREACHES LOVE!

BUT HIS ACTIONS REVEAL IT'S NOT JUST WORDS TO HIM!

EVERYONE!

I AM LEAVING YOU! I AM LEAVING THIS LIFE! YOU MAY FORGET ALL ABOUT ME BY NEXT WEEK!

I WANT YOU TO REMEMBER THIS MAN, THOUGH!

HE IS A MAN WHO REACHES OUT TO PEOPLE WHO ARE NORMALLY HATED!

INSIDE, THEY CELEBRATED. BUT OUTSIDE --

THE PHARISEES LET THEIR DISGUST BE KNOWN...

LOOK AT HIM!

NO SURPRISE THAT HE WOULD ASSOCIATE WITH THOSE TYPES OF PEOPLE!

HE HAS NO SHAME.

IS THERE A PROBLEM?

YES. YOUR TEACHER!

WHY DOES HE SIT AND BREAK BREAD WITH TAX COLLECTORS?

SINNERS!

WE'VE SEEN HIM WITH OTHER SINNERS BEFORE!

LET ME ASK YOU A QUESTION.

WHO NEEDS A DOCTOR? THE HEALTHY? OR THE SICK?

THE SICK, OF COURSE! BUT WHAT --

THEN YOU UNDERSTAND!

I HAVE NOT COME TO CALL THE RIGHTEOUS TO REPENTANCE, FOR IF THEY REALLY ARE RIGHTEOUS THEY ALREADY HAVE REPENTED!

I HAVE COME TO CALL THE SINNERS!

BAH!

GO, NOW, AND LEARN WHAT THIS MEANS: "I DESIRE MERCY, NOT SACRIFICE."

COME, LET US FINISH THIS FEAST YOU HAVE HAD PREPARED FOR US!

HE USED THE WORDS OF THE PROPHET HOSEA TO PUT THE PHARISEES IN THEIR PLACE!

HE HAS AMAZING KNOWLEDGE OF THE SCRIPTURES, AND WISDOM.

I'M SURPRISED YOU KNEW WHAT HE WAS TALKING ABOUT, CONSIDERING YOU'RE A...UH...

CONSIDERING I'M A TAX COLLECTOR?

NOT ANYMORE.

COME, MY NEW FRIENDS, LET'S EAT.

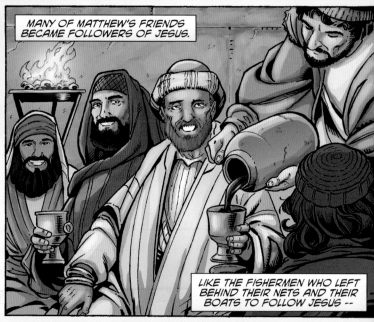

MANY OF MATTHEW'S FRIENDS BECAME FOLLOWERS OF JESUS.

LIKE THE FISHERMEN WHO LEFT BEHIND THEIR NETS AND THEIR BOATS TO FOLLOW JESUS --

-- MATTHEW LEFT BEHIND EVERYTHING.

AND JESUS CHOSE MATTHEW TO BECOME ONE OF THE TWELVE.

MATTHEW WOULD HAVE SEEN JESUS TEACH --

HE WOULD HAVE HEARD JESUS TELL THOSE FANTASTIC, MEANING-FILLED STORIES.

THE PARABLES.

LET HE WHO HAS EARS LISTEN!

THE KINGDOM OF HEAVEN IS LIKE A TREASURE, HIDDEN IN A FIELD!

WHEN A MAN FOUND IT, HE HID IT AGAIN!

AND THEN IN HIS JOY, HE WENT AND SOLD EVERYTHING HE HAD.

AND BOUGHT THAT FIELD!

THE KINGDOM OF HEAVEN IS LIKE A MERCHANT LOOKING FOR FINE PEARLS!

WHEN HE FINDS ONE OF GREAT VALUE, HE'D SELL EVERYTHING HE HAD TO BUY IT, WOULDN'T HE?

HOSANNA!

BLESSED BE HIS NAME!

MATTHEW WOULD HAVE WITNESSED THE PEOPLE WORSHIPING JESUS AND PRAISING HIS NAME AS HE RODE INTO JERUSALEM ON A DONKEY.

AND HE WOULD HAVE RECOGNIZED THE PROPHECY FROM ZECHARIAH: "SEE, YOUR KING COMES TO YOU, GENTLE AND RIDING A DONKEY."

IT IS WRITTEN, "MY HOUSE WILL BE CALLED A 'HOUSE OF PRAYER'" -- BUT YOU HAVE TURNED IT INTO A "DEN OF ROBBERS"!

MATTHEW WOULD HAVE SEEN JESUS' ANGER IN THE TEMPLE AREA AT THE MEN WHO CHEATED PEOPLE WHEN THEY NEEDED TO EXCHANGE MONEY OR BUY DOVES FOR SACRIFICE.

HOSANNA TO THE SON OF DAVID!

WHY, DO YOU HEAR WHAT THESE CHILDREN ARE SAYING?

I DO! HAVEN'T YOU EVER READ, "FROM THE MOUTHS OF CHILDREN YOU HAVE ORDAINED PRAISE"?

HE WOULD HAVE WITNESSED THE RISING CONCERN AND ANGER THE RELIGIOUS LEADERS WOULD HAVE HAD ABOUT JESUS.

BUT DID HE UNDERSTAND WHAT WAS HAPPENING?

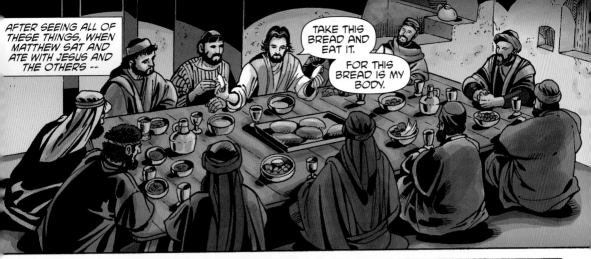

AFTER SEEING ALL OF THESE THINGS, WHEN MATTHEW SAT AND ATE WITH JESUS AND THE OTHERS --

TAKE THIS BREAD AND EAT IT.

FOR THIS BREAD IS MY BODY.

-- HOW COULD HE UNDERSTAND?

HOW COULD ANY OF THEM IMAGINE WHAT WAS ABOUT TO HAPPEN?

DRINK FROM THIS CUP.

THIS IS MY BLOOD. IT IS A COVENANT, POURED OUT FOR YOU.

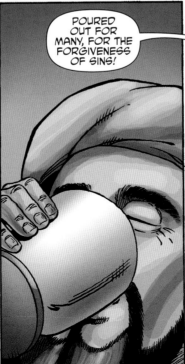

POURED OUT FOR MANY, FOR THE FORGIVENESS OF SINS!

AND NOW I TELL YOU, I WILL NOT DRINK OF THE FRUIT OF THE VINE UNTIL THE DAY WHEN I DRINK IT WITH YOU.

IN MY FATHER'S KINGDOM.

HE COULD NOT KNOW. NONE OF THEM DID.

EVEN THOUGH JESUS HAD ALLUDED TO IT MANY TIMES.

15

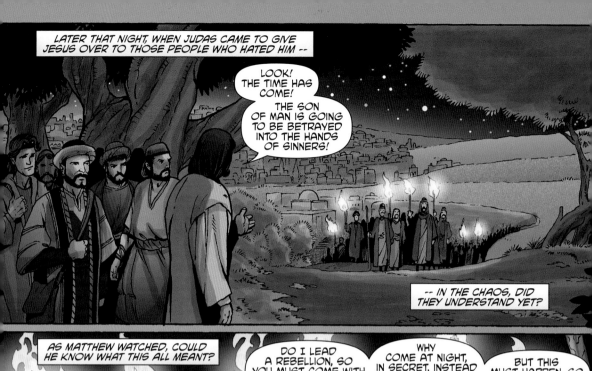

LATER THAT NIGHT, WHEN JUDAS CAME TO GIVE JESUS OVER TO THOSE PEOPLE WHO HATED HIM --

LOOK! THE TIME HAS COME! THE SON OF MAN IS GOING TO BE BETRAYED INTO THE HANDS OF SINNERS!

-- IN THE CHAOS, DID THEY UNDERSTAND YET?

AS MATTHEW WATCHED, COULD HE KNOW WHAT THIS ALL MEANT?

DO I LEAD A REBELLION, SO YOU MUST COME WITH SWORDS AND CLUBS TO CAPTURE ME?

WHY COME AT NIGHT, IN SECRET, INSTEAD OF DURING THE DAY WHEN I WAS TEACHING IN THE TEMPLE COURTS?

BUT THIS MUST HAPPEN, SO SCRIPTURES CAN BE FULFILLED!

WHEN HE CHOSE TO FOLLOW JESUS, MATTHEW'S LIFE HAD CHANGED.

AS HE CHOSE TO RUN AWAY, DID HE UNDERSTAND THAT IT WASN'T JUST HIS LIFE THAT WAS CHANGING --

--THE ENTIRE WORLD WAS GOING TO CHANGE.

WHILE JESUS' BODY WAS BURIED IN A TOMB, SEALED BY A STONE, THE DISCIPLES HID, BEHIND LOCKED DOORS.

EVEN WHEN SOME OF THE WOMEN WHO FOLLOWED JESUS REPORTED HIS TOMB WAS EMPTY, THEY HID.

EVEN WHEN PETER SAW THE TOMB, THEY FEARED.

EVEN WHEN AN ANGEL TOLD THE WOMEN JESUS HAD RISEN, THEY DID NOT UNDERSTAND.

BUT THEN THEY HEARD THAT VOICE.

PEACE BE WITH YOU!

AN IMPOSSIBLE VOICE.

HOW WAS ANYONE HERE? WERE THE DOORS NOT LOCKED?

HOW COULD IT BE HIS VOICE THEY HEAR? WAS THAT VOICE NOT SILENCED?

WHY ARE YOU TROUBLED? WHY DID YOU HAVE DOUBTS!

IT IS ME! I AM NO GHOST!

DO YOU HAVE ANYTHING TO EAT?

AFTER THAT, MATTHEW WOULD HAVE WITNESSED SO MUCH MORE.

THIS TIME, WITH UNDERSTANDING!

LITTLE IS KNOWN ABOUT WHAT HAPPENED TO MATTHEW AFTER THAT POINT.

AS SOMEONE WHO UNDER-STOOD THE SCRIPTURES --

-- AND WHO NOW UNDERSTOOD WHAT JESUS HAD COME TO DO --

-- HE WOULD HAVE TOLD PEOPLE WHAT HE HAD WITNESSED.

"BUT YOU, BETHLEHEM, THOUGH YOU ARE SMALL AMONG THE TRIBES OF JUDAH, OUT OF YOU WILL COME ONE WHO WILL BE RULER OVER ISRAEL."

THIS HAS BEEN FULFILLED IN THE COMING OF JESUS, THE CHRIST!

SOME SAY MATTHEW TRAVELED, AND TOLD OTHER PEOPLE IN OTHER NATIONS ABOUT JESUS AND WHAT HE DID FOR US.

SOME SUGGEST THAT MATTHEW WAS FORCED TO LEAVE, LIKE MANY OF THE OTHER DISCIPLES.

FORCED TO BY THE RELIGIOUS LEADERS OF THE JEWS, WHO WERE NOT HAPPY THAT JESUS' TEACHINGS WERE STILL BEING SPREAD.

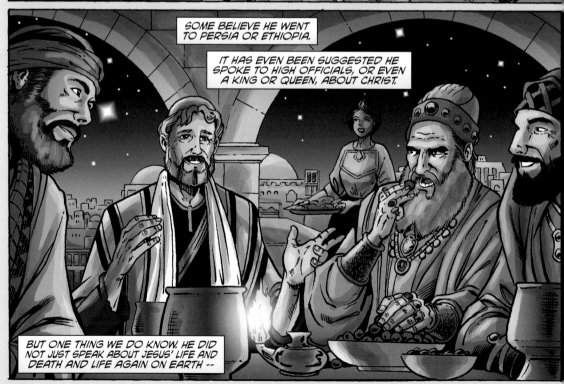

SOME BELIEVE HE WENT TO PERSIA OR ETHIOPIA.

IT HAS EVEN BEEN SUGGESTED HE SPOKE TO HIGH OFFICIALS, OR EVEN A KING OR QUEEN, ABOUT CHRIST.

BUT ONE THING WE DO KNOW. HE DID NOT JUST SPEAK ABOUT JESUS' LIFE AND DEATH AND LIFE AGAIN ON EARTH --

-- HE ALSO WROTE ABOUT IT.

AS AN EDUCATED MAN, MATTHEW WOULD HAVE KNOWN THE VALUE OF PUTTING THE STORY OF THE CHRIST IN WRITING.

AS SOMEONE WHO STUDIED THE JEWISH SCRIPTURES, MATTHEW UNDERSTOOD THE SIGNIFICANCE OF JESUS AND WHAT HE DID.

AS A MAN WHO HAD SPENT TIME WITH JESUS AND THE OTHER DISCIPLES, MATTHEW KNEW ABOUT THEIR STORIES AND EXPERIENCES.

HE WROTE A BOOK ABOUT CHRIST'S LIFE.

WE KNOW HIS BOOK AS THE GOSPEL OF MATTHEW.

WOULD ANYONE EVER EXPECT THIS MAN TO BE INSPIRED BY THE HOLY SPIRIT TO WRITE THIS BOOK?

WASN'T HE A MAN WHO TURNED AGAINST HIS PEOPLE TO SERVE THE ENEMY?

WASN'T HE ONCE A MAN WHOSE JOB NOT ONLY ALLOWED HIM TO CHEAT AND STEAL, BUT IT WAS ALMOST EXPECTED THAT HE WOULD?

AND BECAUSE OF ALL OF THAT, WOULDN'T HE UNDERSTAND THE VALUE OF FOLLOWING CHRIST?

AND THE VALUE OF THE FORGIVENESS OF SINS?

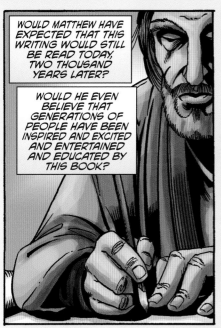

WOULD MATTHEW HAVE EXPECTED THAT THIS WRITING WOULD STILL BE READ TODAY, TWO THOUSAND YEARS LATER?

WOULD HE EVEN BELIEVE THAT GENERATIONS OF PEOPLE HAVE BEEN INSPIRED AND EXCITED AND ENTERTAINED AND EDUCATED BY THIS BOOK?

"SO JOSEPH GOT UP, TOOK THE CHILD AND HIS MOTHER DURING THE NIGHT AND LEFT FOR EGYPT."

"AND SO WAS FULFILLED WHAT THE LORD HAS SAID THROUGH THE PROPHET: 'OUT OF EGYPT I CALLED MY SON.'"

THIS TELLS US THAT HUNDREDS OF YEARS BEFORE JESUS WAS BORN, THE PROPHET HOSEA WROTE ABOUT HIM!

BECAUSE OF THE WAY MATTHEW'S BOOK IS WRITTEN --

-- IT IS THOUGHT THAT HE WROTE HIS BOOK FOR JEWISH PEOPLE.

"ON THE FIRST DAY OF THE FEAST OF UNLEAVENED BREAD, THE DISCIPLES CAME TO JESUS..."

IT EXPLAINS HOW JESUS FULFILLED THEIR PROPHECIES, ESPECIALLY THE PROPHECIES OF THE MESSIAH.

...EVERYTHING JESUS DID WAS ABOUT OUR SIN!

NOT CONDEMNATION, BUT FORGIVENESS!

YOU THERE!

LIKE THE OTHERS, EXACT DETAILS FOR HIS DEATH ARE HARD TO FIND.

THERE ARE DIFFERENT TRADITIONS ABOUT HOW MATTHEW DIED AND WHEN.

SOME SAY HE WAS BURNED AT THE STAKE, SOME SAY HE WAS BEHEADED.

SOME SAY IN EGYPT, SOME SAY IN ETHIOPIA.

BUT THE EARLIEST TRADITIONS SAY HE WAS KILLED BECAUSE OF HIS MINISTRY.

MATTHEW WAS A SINNER WHO GAVE UP HIS SINFUL LIFE, AND ALL ITS ADVANTAGES.

BUT HE DID NOT JUST GIVE UP MONEY WHEN HE FOLLOWED JESUS.

AS A MAN WHO WORKED WITH MONEY, HE UNDERSTOOD VALUE.

HE UNDERSTOOD JESUS WAS SOMEONE WORTH LIVING FOR.

HE GAVE UP HIS ENTIRE LIFE, AS THE OTHERS HAD.

HE UNDERSTOOD WORTH.

AND WORTH DYING FOR.

WE SHOULD NOT BE SURPRISED THAT MATTHEW REMEMBERED AND WROTE ABOUT JESUS' STORY ABOUT THE MAN WHO FOUND A TREASURE IN A FIELD AND SOLD EVERYTHING TO BUY THAT FIELD.

THAT STORY DESCRIBED MATTHEW'S LIFE. AND DEATH.

MATTHEW FOUND HIS TREASURE - JESUS CHRIST - AND HE GAVE UP EVERYTHING.

BECAUSE HE KNEW JESUS WAS WORTH EVERYTHING.

MATTHIAS
"The Replacement"

"THEN THEY CAST LOTS,
AND THE LOT FELL
TO MATTHIAS; SO HE
WAS ADDED TO THE
ELEVEN APOSTLES."
ACTS 1:26 (NIV)

NAME: MATTHIAS

FAMILY: UNKNOWN

OCCUPATION: UNKNOWN

THIS IS THE STORY OF A MAN...

...WHOSE ENTIRE LIFE IS A MYSTERY TO US.

IN TRUTH, WE ONLY KNOW TWO THINGS ABOUT THIS MAN.

BROTHERS! SISTERS!

IT HAS BEEN A FEW DAYS SINCE JESUS TOLD US TO RETURN HERE TO JERUSALEM.

HE HAS RETURNED TO HEAVEN, BUT HAS SAID HE WOULD SEND HIS HOLY SPIRIT.

WE HAVE SPENT MUCH TIME TOGETHER IN PRAYER.

WE KNOW HE WAS A FOLLOWER OF JESUS FROM THE BEGINNING.

AND WE KNOW HIS NAME – MATTHIAS.

THERE IS SOMETHING I FEEL I MUST BRING UP.

THERE IS ONE WHO IS NO LONGER WITH US.

WE KNOW HIS NAME ONLY BECAUSE OF ANOTHER MAN'S ACTIONS.

JUDAS! IN HIS ACTIONS, THE WORDS OF SCRIPTURE HAVE BEEN FULFILLED!

HE WAS ONE OF US, A FRIEND, SHARING JESUS' MINISTRY WITH US.

BUT HE BETRAYED JESUS!

AND MATTHIAS'S STORY IS REMEMBERED BECAUSE IT IS FOREVER LINKED TO JUDAS'S STORY.

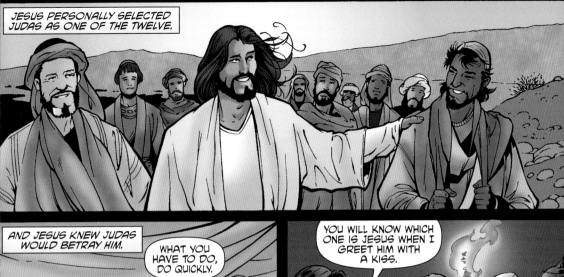

JESUS PERSONALLY SELECTED JUDAS AS ONE OF THE TWELVE.

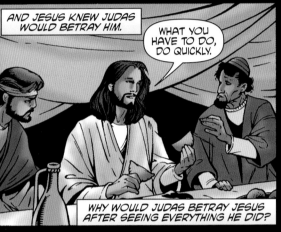

AND JESUS KNEW JUDAS WOULD BETRAY HIM.

WHAT YOU HAVE TO DO, DO QUICKLY.

WHY WOULD JUDAS BETRAY JESUS AFTER SEEING EVERYTHING HE DID?

YOU WILL KNOW WHICH ONE IS JESUS WHEN I GREET HIM WITH A KISS.

YOUR PAYMENT.

WAS IT GREED? DISILLUSIONMENT? DISAPPOINTMENT?

WAS HE DECEIVED BY SATAN? POSSESSED BY SATAN?

JUDAS, ARE YOU BETRAYING ME WITH A KISS?

WE MAY NOT KNOW WHY HE DID IT, BUT AFTER HE DID...

I HAVE BETRAYED INNOCENT BLOOD!

WHAT'S THAT TO US?

IT'S ON YOU IF YOU BELIEVE THAT.

...HE REALIZED HIS SIN AND TOOK HIS LIFE.

HE PUNISHED HIMSELF FOR BETRAYING THE MAN WHO WOULD DIE...

...TO FORGIVE OUR SINS.

AND THE NUMBER OF APOSTLES WENT FROM TWELVE TO ELEVEN.

SO NOW HE IS GONE! THE LAND HIS MONEY BOUGHT IS A DEAD PLACE.

THIS FULFILLS THE SCRIPTURE DAVID WROTE, INSPIRED BY THE HOLY SPIRIT:

"MAY HIS HOME BE DESERTED; LET NO ONE DWELL IN IT."

BUT DAVID WROTE ANOTHER SCRIPTURE TO BE FULFILLED, TOO.

"MAY SOMEONE ELSE TAKE HIS POSITION OF LEADERSHIP."

WHOEVER THAT PERSON IS, HE SHOULD BE ONE OF US WHO WAS THERE FROM THE BEGINNING TO THE END.

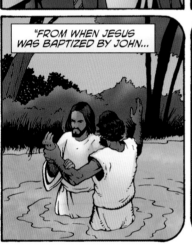

"FROM WHEN JESUS WAS BAPTIZED BY JOHN...

"...TO THE DAYS AFTER CHRIST RETURNED TO US, ALIVE...

"...TO THE DAY HE ASCENDED INTO HEAVEN!"

TWO MEN FIT THIS DESCRIPTION – MATTHIAS AND BARSABBAS.

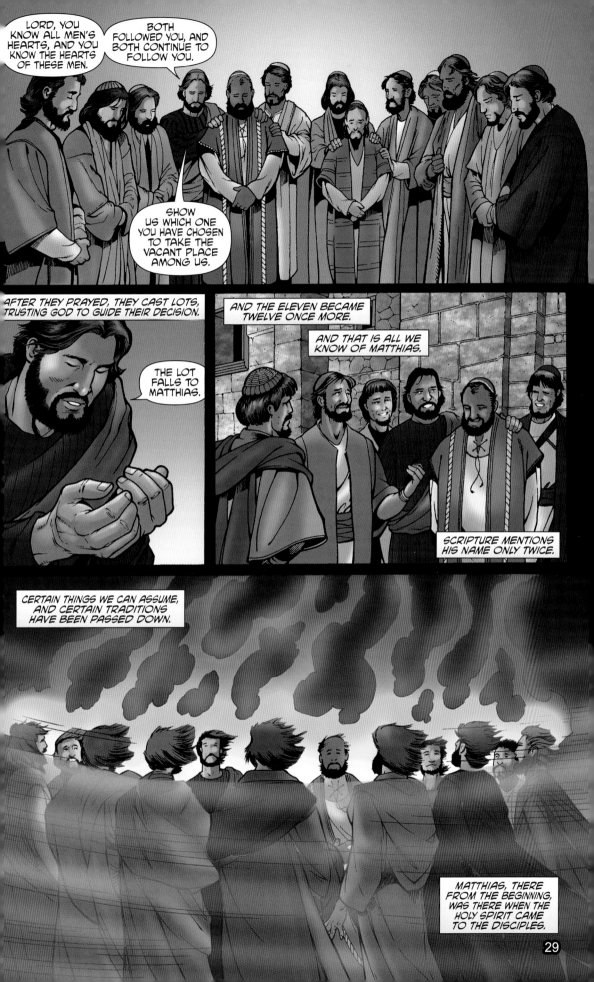

AFTER THAT?

LIKE THE OTHER APOSTLES - HE LEFT TO GO SHARE THE INCREDIBLE NEWS OF THE RESURRECTION WITH THOSE WHO HAD NOT HEARD THE STORY.

THE MESSIAH THAT THE PROPHET SPEAKS OF CAME!

JESUS OF NAZARETH FULFILLED THESE PROPHESIES.

HE WOULD MOST LIKELY HAVE PREACHED AND TAUGHT ABOUT JESUS TO THE JEWS OUTSIDE OF JUDEA.

TRADITIONS GIVE DIFFERENT ACCOUNTS OF HIS DEATH.

THE MOST RELIABLE SUGGEST THAT HE RETURNED TO JERUSALEM.

IN JERUSALEM, HE UPSET THE RELIGIOUS LEADERS BY SPREADING THE GOSPEL.

THE DIFFERENT TRADITIONS MAY NOT AGREE ABOUT WHERE OR HOW...

...BUT THEY AGREE THAT LIKE THE OTHER ELEVEN, HE DEDICATED HIS LIFE TO CHRIST.

AND HE DIED FOR CHRIST, TOO.

TWO MEN. TWO STORIES WITH THE SAME BEGINNING - FOLLOWING CHRIST.

ONE MAN DIED IN SERVICE TO HIMSELF...

... THE OTHER, IN SERVICE TO CHRIST.

TWO STORIES WITH TWO VERY DIFFERENT ENDINGS.

JOHN
"The Beloved Disciple"

THE REVELATION FROM JESUS CHRIST, WHICH GOD GAVE HIM TO SHOW HIS SERVANTS WHAT MUST SOON TAKE PLACE. HE MADE IT KNOWN BY SENDING HIS ANGEL TO HIS SERVANT JOHN, WHO TESTIFIES TO EVERYTHING HE SAW—THAT IS, THE WORD OF GOD AND THE TESTIMONY OF JESUS CHRIST.
REVELATION 1:1-2 (NIV)

NAME: JOHN, ONE OF THE "SONS OF THUNDER"

FAMILY: YOUNGER BROTHER OF JAMES; SON OF ZEBEDEE; POSSIBLY THE UNCLE OF JUDAS, KNOWN AS THADDAEUS

CONNECTIONS TO OTHER APOSTLES: CLOSE FRIEND OF THE OTHER FISHERMEN, PARTICULARLY PETER AND ANDREW

OCCUPATION: FISHERMAN

WHEN JOHN WROTE DOWN HIS ACCOUNT OF THE LIFE OF CHRIST, HE DIDN'T START WITH JESUS' BIRTH.

HE STARTED WITH THE BEGINNING OF EVERYTHING.

"IN THE BEGINNING WAS THE WORD.

"AND THE WORD WAS WITH GOD.

"AND THE WORD WAS GOD.

"THE WORD BECAME FLESH.

"AND DWELLED AMONG US.

"WE HAVE WITNESSED HIS GLORY.

"THE GLORY OF THE ONLY SON.

"THE SON WHO CAME FROM THE FATHER, FULL OF GRACE AND TRUTH.

"OUT OF HIS FULL- NESS WE HAVE ALL RECEIVED GRACE.

"NO ONE HAS SEEN GOD BUT THE SON.

"AND THROUGH THE SON, THE FATHER HAS BEEN MADE KNOWN."

JOHN, THE YOUNGER BROTHER OF JAMES.

ONE OF JESUS' TRIO OF CLOSE DISCIPLES.

AN EYE WITNESS TO JESUS' LIFE...

...AND A WRITER OF JESUS' LIFE STORY.

LIKE ANDREW, JOHN WAS FIRST A DISCIPLE OF JOHN THE BAPTIST.

ABOUT THE BAPTIST, JOHN WROTE:

"THERE CAME A MAN, SENT BY GOD...AS A WITNESS TO THE LIGHT...

"HE WAS NOT THE LIGHT, BUT ONLY A WITNESS TO THE LIGHT."

LOOK THERE!

THE LAMB OF GOD, WHO TAKES AWAY THE WORLD'S SINS.

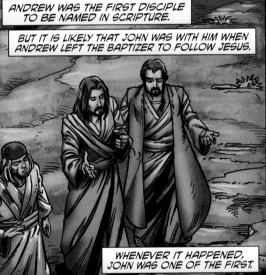

ANDREW WAS THE FIRST DISCIPLE TO BE NAMED IN SCRIPTURE.

BUT IT IS LIKELY THAT JOHN WAS WITH HIM WHEN ANDREW LEFT THE BAPTIZER TO FOLLOW JESUS.

WHENEVER IT HAPPENED, JOHN WAS ONE OF THE FIRST.

LIKE ANDREW, HE TOLD HIS OLDER BROTHER ABOUT JESUS.

HE SPOKE WITH SUCH WISDOM! WISDOM THAT CAME FROM TRUTH AND KNOW-LEDGE.

SIMON, HOW WAS YOUR CATCH?

WE CAUGHT NOTHING, ZEBEDEE.

LATER THAT DAY...

HELP! THERE'S TOO MUCH!

THAT'S SIMON...

WHAT'S GOING ON?

THEY'VE PUT OUT THEIR NETS.

AT THIS HOUR?

JOHN WITNESSED SOME THINGS THAT THE OTHER APOSTLES DID NOT.

THIS IS MY SON.

WITH HIM I AM WELL PLEASED.

LISTEN TO WHAT HE SAYS.

HE SAW JESUS' TRANSFIGURATION AND HEARD THE VOICE OF GOD.

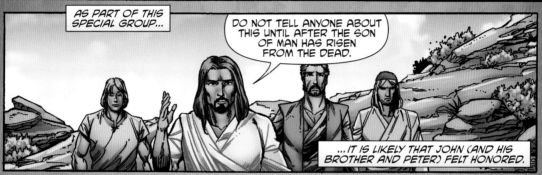

AS PART OF THIS SPECIAL GROUP...

DO NOT TELL ANYONE ABOUT THIS UNTIL AFTER THE SON OF MAN HAS RISEN FROM THE DEAD.

...IT IS LIKELY THAT JOHN (AND HIS BROTHER AND PETER) FELT HONORED.

LATER...

I COMMAND THIS DEMON TO LEAVE THIS MAN.

LEAVE HIM, IN THE NAME OF JESUS!

WHO IS THAT?

WHAT ARE YOU DOING?

YOU DARE SPEAK IN THE NAME OF JESUS?

WHO ARE YOU TO DO THAT?

DID THE MASTER GIVE YOU THIS AUTHORITY?

DID THE TEACHER TELL YOU TO DO THIS?

I... NO... BUT...

LET US TAKE CARE OF THIS!

LATER, AN ARGUMENT BROKE OUT AMONG THE DISCIPLES ABOUT WHO WOULD BE GREATEST.

WHAT WERE YOU ARGUING ABOUT ON THE ROAD?

NO ONE WANTED TO ANSWER.

OF COURSE, JESUS KNEW.

ANYONE WHO WANTS TO BE FIRST MUST BE LAST.

HE MUST BE THE SERVANT OF ALL.

TRUTHFULLY, UNLESS YOU BECOME LIKE A CHILD, YOU WON'T EVEN ENTER THE KINGDOM.

THE ONE WHO HUMBLES HIMSELF LIKE THIS CHILD IS THE GREATEST IN THE KINGDOM OF HEAVEN.

AND IF YOU WELCOME A CHILD LIKE THIS IN MY NAME...

...YOU ARE WELCOMING ME...

...AND THE ONE WHO SENT ME.

WHOEVER IS LEAST AMONG YOU WILL BE THE GREATEST.

MASTER! I NEED TO TELL YOU SOMETHING.

THE OTHER DAY WE SAW A MAN CASTING OUT DEMONS IN YOUR NAME.

WE TRIED TO STOP HIM, BECAUSE HE WASN'T ONE OF US.

DO NOT STOP HIM.

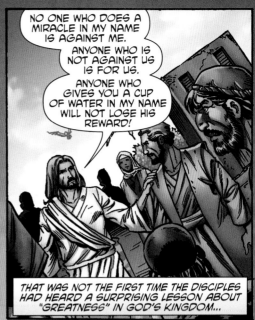

NO ONE WHO DOES A MIRACLE IN MY NAME IS AGAINST ME.

ANYONE WHO IS NOT AGAINST US IS FOR US.

ANYONE WHO GIVES YOU A CUP OF WATER IN MY NAME WILL NOT LOSE HIS REWARD!

THAT WAS NOT THE FIRST TIME THE DISCIPLES HAD HEARD A SURPRISING LESSON ABOUT "GREATNESS" IN GOD'S KINGDOM...

...AND IT WAS NOT THE LAST.

THE TOWN HAS NO PLACE FOR YOU TO STAY!

DO YOU WANT US TO CALL DOWN FIRE ON THEM LIKE ELIJAH DID?

DO YOU KNOW WHAT YOU ARE SAYING?

THE SON OF MAN COMES NOT TO DESTROY MEN'S LIVES, BUT TO SAVE THEM.

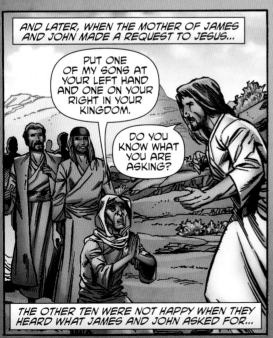

AND LATER, WHEN THE MOTHER OF JAMES AND JOHN MADE A REQUEST TO JESUS...

PUT ONE OF MY SONS AT YOUR LEFT HAND AND ONE ON YOUR RIGHT IN YOUR KINGDOM.

DO YOU KNOW WHAT YOU ARE ASKING?

THE OTHER TEN WERE NOT HAPPY WHEN THEY HEARD WHAT JAMES AND JOHN ASKED FOR...

...SO ONCE MORE JESUS EXPLAINED WHAT IT MEANT TO BE IN HIS KINGDOM.

WHOEVER WANTS TO BE GREAT MUST BE A SERVANT.

THE SON OF MAN DID NOT COME TO BE SERVED.

I CAME TO SERVE OTHERS AND TO GIVE MY LIFE AS THE RANSOM FOR MANY!

NOT LONG AFTERWARD, THE TWELVE LEARNED WHAT HE MEANT.

GETHSEMANE.

JESUS AND THE DISCIPLES ATE TOGETHER AND THEN CAME TO THIS PLACE.

THE DISCIPLES HAD NO IDEA WHAT WAS ABOUT TO HAPPEN.

KEEP WATCH AND PRAY. MY SOUL ACHES.

TWICE, JESUS FOUND THEM SLEEPING AND REBUKED THEM.

THE THIRD TIME WOULD BE THE LAST.

WAKE UP! GET UP! MY BETRAYER APPROACHES.

JUDAS ISCARIOT KNEW THIS WAS A PLACE JESUS LIKED TO PRAY.

HE LED SOLDIERS AND SERVANTS OF THE CHIEF PRIESTS TO ARREST JESUS.

THE DISCIPLES SCATTERED.

ALL BUT TWO.

WHERE ARE THEY GOING?

THE HIGH PRIEST'S HOME, I THINK.

I THINK I CAN GET US IN TO SEE WHAT'S HAPPENING.

THE HIGH PRIEST KNOWS MY FAMILY. HIS SERVANTS WILL ALLOW US INSIDE.

I'M GOING TO GET A CLOSER LOOK.

I'LL WAIT OVER HERE.

ARE YOU THE CHRIST?

BY OATH TO THE LIVING GOD, TELL ME!

ARE YOU THE CHRIST, THE SON OF GOD?

JOHN DID NOT SEE PETER AGAIN UNTIL AFTER EVERYTHING WAS FINISHED.

I AM.

AND IN THE FUTURE YOU WILL SEE THE SON OF MAN...

...IN THE CLOUDS OF HEAVEN, SITTING AT THE RIGHT HAND OF GOD.

BLASPHEMY!

DO YOU NEED MORE WITNESSES?

HIS OWN BLASPHEMY CONDEMNS HIM!

DEATH IS THE ONLY PUNISHMENT.

YES, DEATH!

CRUCIFY HIM! HE DESERVES DEATH!

JESUS WAS SHUFFLED FROM COURT TO COURT.

CONDEMNATION CAME FROM THE RELIGIOUS LEADERS.

BUT CRUCIFIXION COULD COME ONLY FROM THE ROMAN LEADERS.

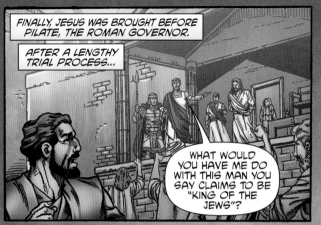

FINALLY, JESUS WAS BROUGHT BEFORE PILATE, THE ROMAN GOVERNOR.

AFTER A LENGTHY TRIAL PROCESS...

WHAT WOULD YOU HAVE ME DO WITH THIS MAN YOU SAY CLAIMS TO BE "KING OF THE JEWS"?

CRUCIFY HIM!

NO.

CRUCIFY HIM!

EVENTUALLY, PILATE GAVE IN.

THE ROMANS BEAT AND MOCKED JESUS, AND THEN HAD HIM CARRY HIS OWN CROSS.

THIS CAN'T BE HAPPENING!

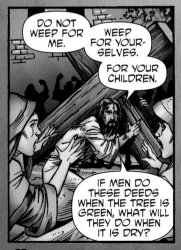

DO NOT WEEP FOR ME. WEEP FOR YOURSELVES. FOR YOUR CHILDREN.

IF MEN DO THESE DEEDS WHEN THE TREE IS GREEN, WHAT WILL THEY DO WHEN IT IS DRY?

MARY!

YOU SHOULD NOT SEE THIS.

HE IS MY SON!

40

JESUS WAS NAILED TO THE CROSS AND LIFTED UP.

JOHN WATCHED WITH JESUS' MOTHER.

CLOSER. I WANT TO SEE HIS FACE...

...AND HEAR HIS VOICE...

...ONE LAST TIME.

DEAR WOMAN...

HERE IS YOUR SON.

AND HERE IS YOUR MOTHER.

AFTER THAT DAY, JOHN TOOK MARY, JESUS' MOTHER, INTO HIS OWN HOME.

FINALLY, AFTER HOURS OF SUFFERING...

IT IS FINISHED!

AND HE BREATHED HIS LAST.

A MAN NAMED JOSEPH OF ARIMATHEA RECEIVED PERMISSION TO BURY JESUS' BODY.

SOME OF US ARE GOING TO FOLLOW.

WE WANT TO SEE HOW THEY TAKE CARE OF HIM.

JOHN REJOINED THE OTHERS IN HIDING FRIDAY NIGHT AND SATURDAY.

BUT SATURDAY MORNING...

SOMEONE'S COMING!

PETER! JOHN! JESUS' TOMB IS EMPTY!

WHO TOOK HIM?

NO ONE. AN ANGEL SPOKE TO ME...

...AND SAID, "WHY ARE YOU LOOKING FOR THE LIVING AMONG THE DEAD?"

THEY REMEMBERED HIS WORDS.

CAN IT BE?

I DON'T BELIEVE IT.

"ON THE THIRD DAY, THE SON OF MAN WILL RISE FROM THE DEAD."

WHAT ARE YOU WAITING FOR, JOHN?

WHAT DO YOU SEE?

NOTHING. JUST LIKE SHE SAID.

GET IN HERE!

42

IT'S TRUE!

HE SAW.

AND BELIEVED.

JOHN WROTE ABOUT THESE THINGS IN HIS OWN ACCOUNT OF JESUS' LIFE.

"JESUS DID MANY MORE MIRACULOUS SIGNS NOT RECORDED IN THIS BOOK.

"THESE ARE WRITTEN THAT YOU MIGHT BELIEVE...

"IF EVERYTHING JESUS DID WAS WRITTEN DOWN, THE WHOLE WORLD WOULD NOT HAVE ROOM FOR THE BOOKS."

IT IS INTERESTING TO NOTE THAT JOHN, WHO WISHED TO BE HONORED ABOVE THE OTHERS...

...NEVER ONCE USED HIS OWN NAME IN HIS BOOK.

HE SIMPLY CALLED HIMSELF "THE DISCIPLE"...

...OR "THE ONE JESUS LOVED."

OVER TIME, HE BECAME AN IMPORTANT LEADER, FOUNDING A NUMBER OF CHURCHES.

ONE BY ONE, THE OTHER DISCIPLES DIED AS MARTYRS.

JOHN FACED PERSECUTION. HE WAS ARRESTED AND EXILED AT ONE POINT.

HISTORIANS REPORT HE SURVIVED BEING BOILED IN OIL; HOWEVER HE DID NOT DIE A VIOLENT DEATH.

DURING HIS EXILE TO THE ISLAND OF PATMOS, JOHN HAD A VISION.

HE RECORDED HIS VISION IN THE BOOK NOW CALLED "REVELATION".

"THE REVELATION FROM JESUS CHRIST, GIVEN BY GOD TO SHOW HIS SERVANTS WHAT MUST TAKE PLACE.

"HE REVEALED IT BY SENDING AN ANGEL TO JOHN, HIS SERVANT...

"BLESSED ARE THOSE WHO HEAR IT AND TAKE IT TO HEART... BECAUSE THE TIME IS NEAR..."

THIS BOOK IS FULL OF SYMBOLS AND PROMISES.

IT REVEALS GOD'S PLAN FOR THE WORLD.

AND EVEN WITH ITS STRANGE AND TERRIFYING SYMBOLS, IT GIVES COMFORT.

THE COMFORT OF GOD'S LOVE.

THE COMFORT THAT JESUS LIVES AND WILL RETURN.

"HE WHO TESTIFIES TO THESE THINGS SAYS, 'YES, I AM COMING SOON!'

"AMEN. COME, LORD JESUS.

"THE GRACE OF THE LORD JESUS CHRIST BE WITH HIS PEOPLE. AMEN."

JOHN'S WRITINGS ENCOMPASS THE ENTIRETY OF HISTORY.

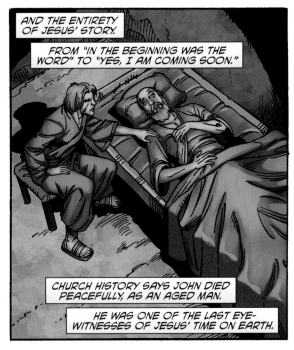

AND THE ENTIRETY OF JESUS' STORY.

FROM "IN THE BEGINNING WAS THE WORD" TO "YES, I AM COMING SOON."

CHURCH HISTORY SAYS JOHN DIED PEACEFULLY, AS AN AGED MAN.

HE WAS ONE OF THE LAST EYE-WITNESSES OF JESUS' TIME ON EARTH.

SIMON
"The Zealot"

"WHEN THEY ARRIVED THEY
WENT UPSTAIRS TO THE
ROOM WHERE THEY WERE
STAYING. THOSE PRESENT
WERE PETER, JOHN, JAMES
AND ANDREW; PHILIP AND
THOMAS, BARTHOLOMEW
AND MATTHEW; JAMES
SON OF ALPHAEUS AND
SIMON THE ZEALOT, AND
JUDAS SON OF JAMES."
ACTS 1:13 (NIV)

NAME: SIMON,
ALSO KNOWN AS
"THE ZEALOT" OR
"THE CANAANITE"
(WHICH CAN ALSO
MEAN "ZEALOUS")

OCCUPATION:
UNKNOWN, ALTHOUGH
HE WAS LIKELY A
MEMBER OF A VIOLENT
POLITICAL GROUP
CALLED ZEALOTS

FOR 400 YEARS, THE JEWISH PEOPLE HAD LIVED UNDER THE RULE OF OTHER KINGDOMS.

AND FOR 400 YEARS, THEY HAD WAITED FOR A MESSIAH, THE PROMISED SAVIOR.

JUDAS THE GALILEAN AND HIS FOLLOWERS, THE ZEALOTS, REBELLED VIOLENTLY AGAINST ROME, THE CURRENT RULING KINGDOM.

THE REBELLION WAS CRUSHED. JUDAS WAS KILLED, AND HIS SONS WERE CRUCIFIED.

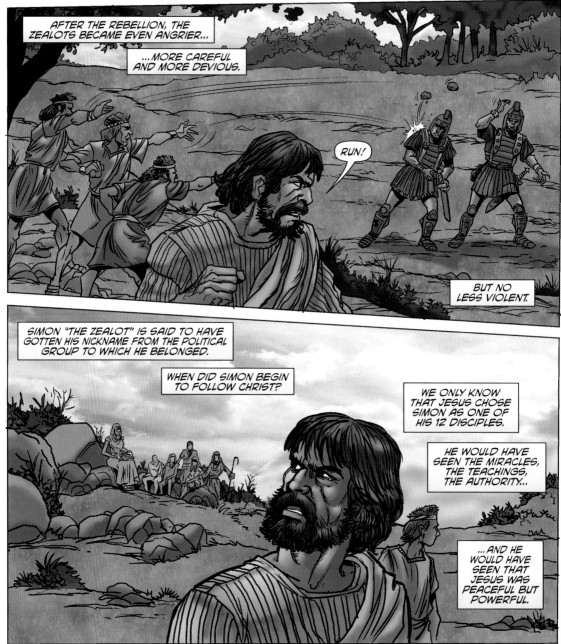

AFTER THE REBELLION, THE ZEALOTS BECAME EVEN ANGRIER...

...MORE CAREFUL AND MORE DEVIOUS.

RUN!

BUT NO LESS VIOLENT.

SIMON "THE ZEALOT" IS SAID TO HAVE GOTTEN HIS NICKNAME FROM THE POLITICAL GROUP TO WHICH HE BELONGED.

WHEN DID SIMON BEGIN TO FOLLOW CHRIST?

WE ONLY KNOW THAT JESUS CHOSE SIMON AS ONE OF HIS 12 DISCIPLES.

HE WOULD HAVE SEEN THE MIRACLES, THE TEACHINGS, THE AUTHORITY...

...AND HE WOULD HAVE SEEN THAT JESUS WAS PEACEFUL BUT POWERFUL.

SURELY, JESUS WAS THE MESSIAH! THE PROMISED SAVIOR!

THINK NOT THAT I AM COME TO SEND PEACE ON EARTH: I CAME NOT TO SEND PEACE, BUT A SWORD.

FOR SOMEONE LIKE SIMON, WHO WANTED HIS NATION AND HIS PEOPLE TO BE FREE FROM ROME...

...THIS IS WHAT HE HAD BEEN WAITING FOR!

OR WAS IT?

LIKE THE OTHERS, SIMON MISUNDER-STOOD WHAT JESUS HAD COME TO DO...

...WHAT THE SAVIOR HAD COME TO SAVE HIS PEOPLE FROM.

AFTER JESUS REAPPEARED TO THEM, LEAVING BEHIND THE EMPTY TOMB...

...THE DISCIPLES BEGAN TO UNDERSTAND WHAT HE HAD BEEN SAYING.

HE HAD NOT COME JUST TO SAVE THE JEWS.

THOMAS
"The Doubter"

"THEN HE SAID TO THOMAS,
'PUT YOUR FINGER HERE, AND
SEE MY HANDS; AND PUT
OUT YOUR HAND, AND PLACE
IT IN MY SIDE. DO NOT
DISBELIEVE, BUT BELIEVE.'"
JOHN 20:27 (ESV)

NAME: THOMAS,
ALSO KNOWN AS
DIDYMUS, WHICH
MEANS "THE TWIN"

FAMILY: POSSIBLY A
TWIN BROTHER OR
SISTER, CONSIDERING
HIS NICKNAME, BUT
THERE IS NO RECORD

OCCUPATION: MOST
LIKELY A FISHERMAN

WE CALL HIM "THOMAS THE DOUBTER" OR "DOUBTING THOMAS"...

...BUT THAT'S NOT COMPLETELY FAIR.

WE DO NOT KNOW WHAT THOMAS WAS DOING WHEN HE MET JESUS.

IT IS LIKELY THAT HE WAS A FISHERMAN FROM THE SAME AREA AS THE OTHERS.

IF SO, HE WOULD HAVE LEARNED ABOUT JESUS FROM THEM.

WE DO NOT KNOW WHEN THOMAS BEGAN TO FOLLOW JESUS...

...BUT WE DO KNOW THAT HE WAS ONE OF THE 12 DISCIPLES JESUS CHOSE.

AND HE DID NOT DOUBT.

HE TRUSTED JESUS ENOUGH TO DROP EVERYTHING AND FOLLOW HIM.

WOULD "THOMAS THE DEDICATED" BE ANOTHER NAME WE COULD GIVE HIM?

CONSIDER HIS LOYALTY WHEN JESUS WAS PERSECUTED.

IN JERUSALEM, IN THE AREA OF THE TEMPLE, SOME JEWS CONFRONTED JESUS:

IF YOU'RE THE CHRIST – THE MESSIAH – JUST SAY IT!

I DID, BUT YOU WOULD NOT BELIEVE.

MY FATHER IS GREATER THAN ALL.

I HAVE DONE MIRACLES IN MY FATHER'S NAME.

I AND THE FATHER ARE ONE.

THEY INTENDED TO SEIZE JESUS AND STONE HIM.

I HAVE SHOWN YOU MANY MIRACLES FROM THE FATHER.

WHICH MIRACLE ARE YOU STONING ME FOR?

IT'S NOT FOR THE MIRACLES. IT'S FOR THE BLASPHEMY!

YOU ACCUSE ME OF BLASPHEMY FOR SAYING, "I AM GOD'S SON"?

YOU MAY NOT BELIEVE MY WORDS.

BUT BELIEVE THE MIRACLES THAT YOU MAY KNOW THIS.

THE FATHER IS IN ME, AND I AM IN THE FATHER.

JESUS LEFT THAT AREA.

AND EVEN THOUGH JESUS MADE THESE BOLD STATEMENTS THAT MANY DID NOT BELIEVE...

... THOMAS FOLLOWED HIM. HE DID NOT DOUBT JESUS' MESSAGE.

MAYBE ANOTHER NAME FOR HIM COULD BE "THOMAS THE DUTIFUL."

JESUS! MARY AND MARTHA HAVE SENT US!

THEIR BROTHER, LAZARUS, IS DEATHLY ILL.

THIS ILLNESS WILL NOT END IN DEATH.

IT IS HAPPENING FOR GOD'S GLORY, SO THAT GOD'S SON MAY BE GLORIFIED THROUGH IT.

JESUS STAYED WHERE THEY WERE FOR TWO MORE DAYS.

AND THEN...

IT IS TIME FOR US TO RETURN TO JUDEA.

BUT MASTER, YOU KNOW THEY WANT TO KILL YOU THERE!

AND YOU WANT TO GO BACK?

OUR FRIEND LAZARUS HAS FALLEN ASLEEP.

I AM GOING THERE TO WAKE HIM UP.

IF HE'S SLEEPING, THEN HE'LL WAKE UP ON HIS OWN.

HE'LL GET BETTER.

WHY PUT YOURSELF AND US IN DANGER?

LAZARUS IS DEAD, MY FRIENDS.

AND I AM GLAD I WAS NOT THERE, SO YOU MAY BELIEVE.

COME, LET US GO TO HIM.

IT WAS THOMAS WHO SPOKE UP.

IF JESUS IS GOING...

...LET US GO, TOO. EVEN IF IT MEANS WE MIGHT DIE WITH HIM.

HE'S RIGHT. LET'S GO!

THOMAS DID NOT DOUBT THAT HE COULD DIE FOLLOWING JESUS.

BUT HE STILL FOLLOWED WHERE JESUS LED.

AND HE WITNESSED A GREAT MIRACLE.

LAZARUS! COME FORTH!

THIS MIRACLE CAUSED THE RELIGIOUS LEADERS TO INTENSIFY THEIR EFFORTS TO STOP JESUS.

COULD WE CALL HIM "THOMAS THE DISTRESSED"?

FOR THE PASSOVER FEAST, JESUS SUPPED WITH HIS DISCIPLES...

...A MEAL THAT, BECAUSE OF THOSE RELIGIOUS LEADERS, BECAME KNOWN AS THE LAST SUPPER.

IT MAY HAVE SEEMED THAT THOMAS DOUBTED JESUS' WORDS THAT NIGHT.

BUT DID HE SPEAK FROM DOUBT?

I AM ONLY GOING TO BE WITH YOU A LITTLE WHILE LONGER.

YOU WILL LOOK FOR ME, AND JUST LIKE I TOLD THE JEWS BEFORE...

...I SAY TO YOU, WHERE I AM GOING YOU CANNOT COME.

LORD, WHERE ARE YOU GOING?

I TOLD YOU, YOU CANNOT FOLLOW ME. BUT PETER, YOU WILL FOLLOW ME LATER.

WHILE JESUS SPOKE TO THE DISCIPLES, WHAT WAS THOMAS THINKING?

"DO NOT LET YOUR HEART BE TROUBLED.

"BELIEVE IN GOD, AND BELIEVE IN ME, ALSO.

"I GO TO PREPARE A PLACE FOR YOU, WHICH MEANS I WILL COME AGAIN.

"SO WHERE I AM, THERE YOU WILL BE, ALSO.

"AND YOU KNOW THE WAY TO WHERE I AM GOING."

WAS IT DOUBT THAT MADE THOMAS SPEAK?

OR DID HE BELIEVE JESUS' WORDS AND SPEAK IN FEAR...

...OF LOSING JESUS?

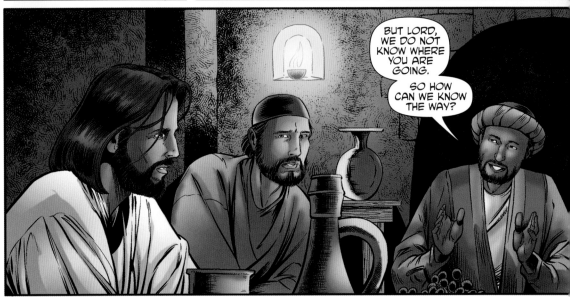

BUT LORD, WE DO NOT KNOW WHERE YOU ARE GOING.

SO HOW CAN WE KNOW THE WAY?

54

I AM THE WAY. I AM THE TRUTH AND THE LIFE.

NO ONE COMES TO THE FATHER EXCEPT THROUGH ME. YOU HAVE KNOWN ME AND YOU HAVE SEEN ME...

...THEREFORE, YOU HAVE KNOWN THE FATHER AND HAVE SEEN THE FATHER.

JESUS SAID MANY THINGS THE DISCIPLES DID NOT UNDERSTAND.

BUT THOMAS UNDERSTOOD THAT JESUS WAS LEAVING THEM.

HE DID NOT DOUBT JESUS WOULD LEAVE THEM...

...EVEN IF HE DID NOT UNDER-STAND WHAT THAT MEANT.

AND WHEN JESUS WAS CRUCIFIED, EVEN THOUGH THOMAS RAN LIKE MOST OF THE OTHERS...

...HE DID NOT DOUBT THAT JESUS HAD DIED.

AFTER THAT DAY, THE DISCIPLES GATHERED AGAIN...

...IN A DARK, LOCKED ROOM, HIDING LIKE SCARED ANIMALS.

BUT THOMAS WAS NOT THERE FOR PART OF THAT TIME.

WHO'S THERE?

IT'S ME! THOMAS!

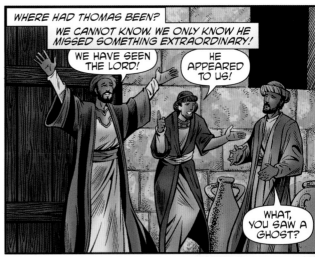

WHERE HAD THOMAS BEEN? WE CANNOT KNOW. WE ONLY KNOW HE MISSED SOMETHING EXTRAORDINARY!

WE HAVE SEEN THE LORD!

HE APPEARED TO US!

WHAT, YOU SAW A GHOST?

NO. HE WAS ALIVE!

HE CAME INTO THIS ROOM EVEN THOUGH THE DOOR AND WINDOWS WERE SEALED.

AND HE WAS ALIVE!

THEN CAME THOMAS'S DEFINING MOMENT.

THIS IS HOW HE BECAME KNOWN AS "DOUBTING THOMAS."

NO. YOU EXPECT ME TO BELIEVE THIS?

NOT UNTIL I CAN SEE HIS HANDS, WITH THE NAIL MARKS!

NOT UNTIL I...I TOUCH THE HOLES THOSE NAILS MADE WITH MY OWN FINGERS!

NOT UNTIL I PUT MY HAND IN HIS SIDE, WHERE THE SPEAR PIERCED HIM!

A WEEK PASSED.

THE DISCIPLES STILL USED THAT ROOM AS THEIR MEETING PLACE.

AND EVEN THOUGH HE DID NOT BELIEVE THEM, THOMAS CONTINUED TO BE WITH THEM.

THEN THEY WERE JOINED BY ANOTHER...

PEACE, FRIENDS!

PEACE TO YOU.

HELLO, THOMAS.

SEE, HERE, MY HANDS.

FEEL MY FLESH AND MY WOUNDS WITH YOUR OWN HANDS.

LOOK, THOMAS...

LOOK, THOMAS, THE WOUND IN MY SIDE.

REACH OUT YOUR HAND.

THOMAS, IT IS TIME TO STOP DOUBTING.

BELIEVE.

OH... MY LORD AND MY GOD!

BECAUSE YOU HAVE SEEN ME, YOU HAVE BELIEVED. BLESSED ARE THOSE WHO HAVE NOT SEEN AND STILL BELIEVE.

AND THOMAS BELIEVED.

PERHAPS THE BEST NAME FOR HIM WOULD BE "THOMAS THE DISCIPLE."

WHEN JESUS LEFT, HE TOLD THEM TO GO TO ALL THE WORLD.

THOMAS TOOK THAT COMMAND SERIOUSLY.

IT IS SAID THAT THOMAS CARRIED CHRIST'S MESSAGE AS FAR AWAY AS INDIA!

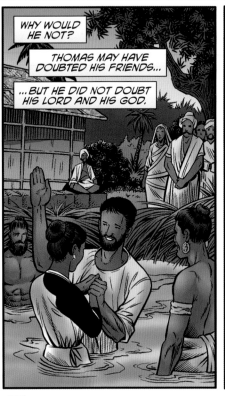

WHY WOULD HE NOT?

THOMAS MAY HAVE DOUBTED HIS FRIENDS...

...BUT HE DID NOT DOUBT HIS LORD AND HIS GOD.

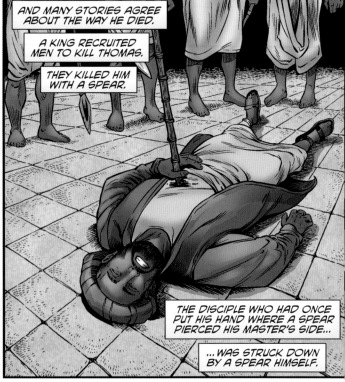

AND MANY STORIES AGREE ABOUT THE WAY HE DIED.

A KING RECRUITED MEN TO KILL THOMAS.

THEY KILLED HIM WITH A SPEAR.

THE DISCIPLE WHO HAD ONCE PUT HIS HAND WHERE A SPEAR PIERCED HIS MASTER'S SIDE...

...WAS STRUCK DOWN BY A SPEAR HIMSELF.

JAMES
"The Lesser"

NAME: JAMES, SON OF ALPHAEUS

FAMILY: ALPHAEUS, FATHER;
MARY, MOTHER (POSSIBLY)

OCCUPATION: UNKNOWN

THERE WERE TWELVE.

OF ALL JESUS' FOLLOWERS, TWELVE WHO HE SELECTED TO BE HIS CLOSE HELPERS.

SOME WE KNOW MUCH ABOUT, LIKE PETER. OR ANDREW. OR EVEN JUDAS.

BUT OTHERS?

WE KNOW VERY LITTLE.

AND ONE OF THESE TWELVE, WE HAVE ONLY A NAME.

JAMES, SON OF ALPHAEUS.

SOME PEOPLE THINK HE WAS MATTHEW'S BROTHER, BECAUSE THEY BOTH HAD FATHERS NAMED ALPHAEUS.

IT'S POSSIBLE, BUT UNLIKELY, BECAUSE WE ARE TOLD ABOUT OTHER BROTHERS IN THIS GROUP--

--BUT THEY ARE NEVER MENTIONED AS BROTHERS.

JESUS, THE PEOPLE ARE HUNGRY. THIS BOY HAS OFFERED HIS LUNCH TO HELP.

"MARY, MOTHER OF JAMES" IS LISTED AMONG SOME OF JESUS' OTHER FOLLOWERS.

WAS SHE THIS JAMES'S MOTHER?

WE CANNOT KNOW FOR SURE.

BUT SOME THINGS WE DO KNOW FOR SURE.

JAMES LEFT EVERYTHING TO FOLLOW JESUS. ALL OF THE TWELVE DID.

HE SAW JESUS PERFORM MIRACLES, JUST LIKE THEY ALL DID.

UNBELIEVABLE! FEEDING EVERYONE WITH THAT SMALL LUNCH!

AFTER ALL THAT, THERE'S STILL BREAD LEFT OVER!

TWELVE BASKETS FULL.

ONE FOR EACH OF US!

HE SERVED IN JESUS' MINISTRY--

--AND JESUS SERVED HIM.

YOU CALL ME TEACHER AND LORD, AND THAT IS WHAT I AM.

NOW THAT I, YOUR LORD, HAVE WASHED YOUR FEET, FOLLOW MY EXAMPLE.

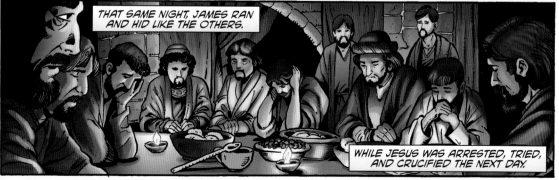

THAT SAME NIGHT, JAMES RAN AND HID LIKE THE OTHERS.

WHILE JESUS WAS ARRESTED, TRIED, AND CRUCIFIED THE NEXT DAY.

HE CELEBRATED WHEN JESUS CAME TO THEM AFTER HIS RESURRECTION.

GO AND PREACH THIS GOOD NEWS TO ALL THE WORLD!

HE WITNESSED JESUS' ASCENSION.

AND HE WAS THERE WHEN THE HOLY SPIRIT FILLED THEM AS JESUS PROMISED.

PERHAPS HE WAS "LESSER," BUT HE WAS A PART OF GOD'S PLAN.

WE DO NOT KNOW HOW HE DIED--

--EARLY TRADITION SUGGESTS HE WAS BEATEN AND STONED FOR PREACHING ABOUT JESUS--

--BUT WE KNOW HOW HE LIVED: IN SERVICE TO JESUS, AND TO THE ONE WHO SENT JESUS.

SIMON PETER
"The Rock"

"SIMON PETER,
A SERVANT AND
APOSTLE OF
JESUS CHRIST..."
2 PETER 1:1 (NIV)

NAME: SIMON, ALSO KNOWN AS
CEPHAS, TRANSLATED AS PETER
(PETER MEANS "LITTLE ROCK")

FAMILY: ANDREW, HIS BROTHER;
HE LIVED WITH HIS WIFE AND
MOTHER-IN-LAW; FATHER, JOHN.

CONNECTIONS TO OTHER APOSTLES:
CLOSE FRIEND TO THE OTHER FISHERMEN,
PARTICULARLY JAMES AND JOHN.

OCCUPATION: FISHERMAN

LATER, AFTER A NIGHT OF WORK THAT BROUGHT IN NO FISH...

SIMON, I NEED YOUR BOAT. WOULD YOU TAKE ME TO WHERE THE PEOPLE CAN SEE ME BETTER?

OF COURSE!

JESUS TAUGHT THE PEOPLE FOR A WHILE.

WHEN FINISHED, HE SPOKE TO SIMON.

NOW, PETER, GO TO THE DEEP WATER AGAIN AND PUT OUT YOUR NETS.

BUT JESUS! WE WERE OUT ALL NIGHT AND CAUGHT NOTHING!

OKAY. IF IT WERE ANYONE ELSE, I'D SAY THEY WERE CRAZY. BUT SINCE IT IS YOU, I'LL DO IT.

68

PETER AND THE OTHERS OF THE TWELVE HELPED JESUS AS HE TRAVELED AND TAUGHT.

ON THE DAY JESUS MIRACULOUSLY FED THOUSANDS, HE ALSO SHOWED THE TWELVE HIS POWER IN A DIFFERENT WAY.

IT'S BEEN A LONG DAY, MY FRIENDS.

GO AHEAD BACK TO CAPERNAUM. I NEED TO FIND A PLACE WHERE I CAN PRAY ALONE.

THE WIND WAS AGAINST THEM.

ROW, MEN! WE WOULD'VE BEEN BETTER OFF WALKING!

I SEE SOMETHING!

DON'T MOCK ME, BROTHER, BUT IT LOOKS LIKE A GHOST!

WHATEVER IT IS, IT'S GAINING ON US!

ROW, MEN! PUT SOME MUSCLE INTO IT!

DON'T BE AFRAID! IT IS ME!

JESUS?

LORD, IS THAT YOU?

LATER, IN CAPERNAUM.

...MY LOVE, SO GOOD TO SEE Y--

I COLLECT THE TEMPLE TAX. DOES YOUR RABBI PAY THAT TAX?

OF COURSE HE DOES!

HMMM. VERY WELL!

I... UH... I NEED TO TALK TO JESUS...

INSIDE, BEFORE PETER HAD A CHANCE TO SPEAK...

SIMON, DO KINGS COLLECT TAXES FROM THEIR OWN SONS, OR FROM OTHERS?

FROM OTHERS.

YES. THE SONS ARE EXEMPT.

BUT, SO WE DO NOT OFFEND, GO TO THE LAKE WITH YOUR POLE--

"--AND CAST YOUR LINE.

"TAKE THE FIRST FISH YOU CATCH.

"OPEN ITS MOUTH. INSIDE, YOU WILL FIND--

"--A FOUR DRACHMA COIN.

"TAKE IT AND PAY MY TEMPLE TAX AND YOURS."

JUST AS HE SAID...

76

COULD YOU NOT KEEP WATCH FOR ONE HOUR?

WATCH AND PRAY THAT YOU WILL NOT FALL INTO TEMPTATION!

YOUR SPIRIT IS WILLING, BUT YOUR BODY?

JESUS RETURNED TO HIS PLACE WHERE HE PRAYED.

...FATHER, MAY YOUR WILL BE DONE...

WHEN HE CAME BACK TO THE TRIO OF APOSTLES...

SIMON?

LORD, I...I... I'M SORRY, LORD.

A THIRD TIME, JESUS PRAYED.

...NOT MY WILL, BUT YOURS BE DONE...

STILL YOU SLEEP? GET UP!

AND A THIRD TIME...

THE HOUR HAS COME.

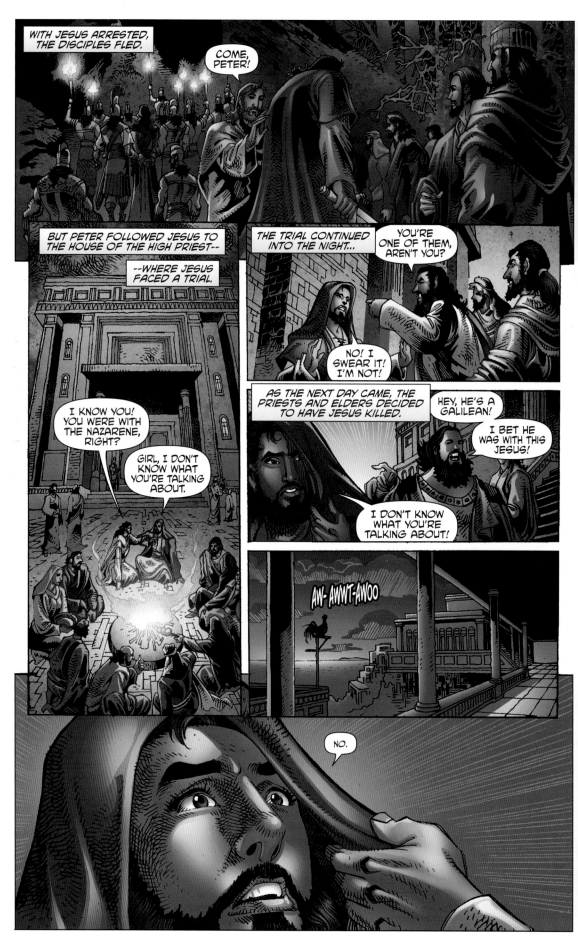

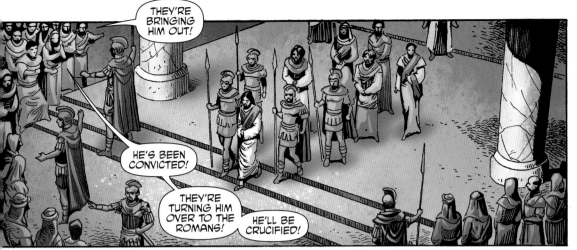

THEY'RE BRINGING HIM OUT!

HE'S BEEN CONVICTED!

THEY'RE TURNING HIM OVER TO THE ROMANS!

HE'LL BE CRUCIFIED!

LIKE THE OTHERS, HE FELL AWAY.

HE WAS NOT THERE FOR THE CRUCIFIXION.

HE WAS NOT THERE FOR THE BURIAL.

IN DARKNESS AND IN FEAR, THEY HID.

THREE DAYS LATER...

PETER? JOHN?

I'VE BEEN TO JESUS' TOMB.

HE'S NOT THERE! AN ANGEL REMINDED US THAT JESUS SAID HE'D RISE AGAIN ON THE THIRD DAY!

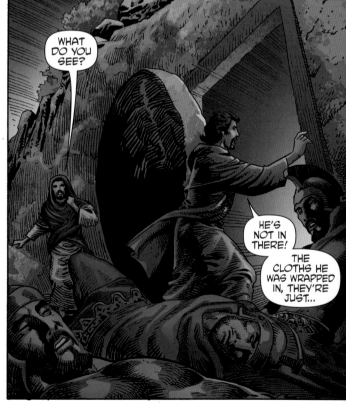

WHAT DO YOU SEE?

HE'S NOT IN THERE! THE CLOTHS HE WAS WRAPPED IN, THEY'RE JUST...

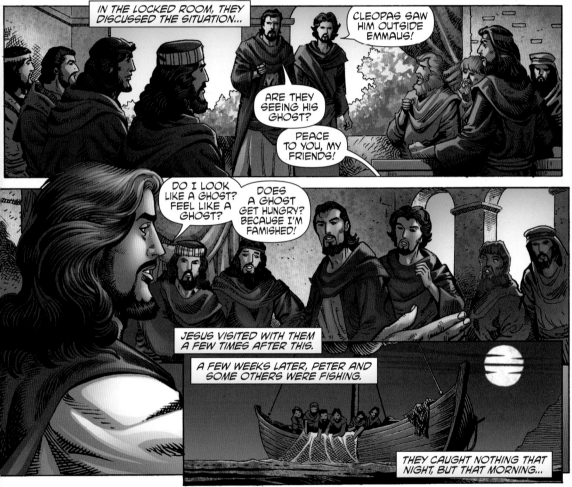

THEY DID SO, AND THIS TIME--

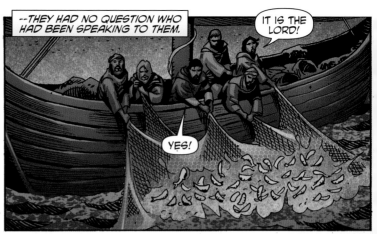

--THEY HAD NO QUESTION WHO HAD BEEN SPEAKING TO THEM.

IT IS THE LORD!

YES!

AND ONCE MORE, PETER JUMPED OUT OF THE BOAT TO GO TO JESUS.

BRING SOME OF YOUR FISH AND JOIN ME FOR BREAKFAST!

AFTER EATING, JESUS TOOK PETER ASIDE.

SIMON, SON OF JOHN, DO YOU LOVE ME EVEN MORE THAN THESE?

YES, LORD, YOU KNOW I LOVE YOU!

THEN FEED MY LAMBS.

SIMON, DO YOU TRULY LOVE ME?

LORD, YES, I YOU KNOW I LOVE YOU.

THEN CARE FOR MY SHEEP.

86

SIMON, SON OF JOHN, DO YOU LOVE ME?

YOU KNOW EVERYTHING, MY LORD.

YOU *KNOW* THAT I LOVE YOU!

THEN FEED MY SHEEP.

PETER, IN YOUR YOUTH, YOU DID AS YOU CHOSE.

YOU DRESSED YOURSELF, AND WENT WHERE YOU PLEASED.

BUT IN YOUR AGE, YOU WILL STRETCH OUT YOUR HAND.

OTHERS WILL DRESS YOU AND YOU WILL GO WHERE THEY TAKE YOU.

...AS I SAID, EVERY-THING WRITTEN ABOUT ME IN THE LAW, PROPHETS, AND PSALMS MUST BE FULFILLED...

JESUS SPENT TIME WITH THEM, UNTIL THE TIME HE ASCENDED INTO HEAVEN.

JESUS TOLD THEM TO WAIT IN JERUSALEM UNTIL THEY WERE FILLED WITH THE HOLY SPIRIT.

WHEN THE HOLY SPIRIT CAME ON THEM, THEY BEGAN TO SPEAK IN TONGUES.

A CROWD GATHERED, AND EVERYONE THE DISCIPLES SPOKE TO HEARD THEM SPEAK IN THEIR OWN LANGUAGE!

SOME WHO HEARD WERE AMAZED, OTHERS SKEPTICAL, THINKING THEY WERE DRUNK!

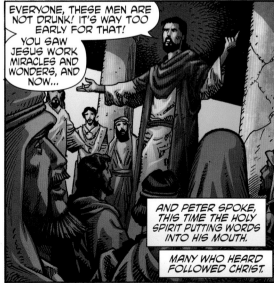

EVERYONE, THESE MEN ARE NOT DRUNK! IT'S WAY TOO EARLY FOR THAT! YOU SAW JESUS WORK MIRACLES AND WONDERS, AND NOW...

AND PETER SPOKE, THIS TIME THE HOLY SPIRIT PUTTING WORDS INTO HIS MOUTH.

MANY WHO HEARD FOLLOWED CHRIST.

FILLED WITH THE SPIRIT, PETER FOLLOWED HIS TEACHER'S EXAMPLE.

ONE DAY, WHEN HE AND JOHN WENT TO THE TEMPLE TO PRAY...

ALMS! GIVE TO THE POOR, PLEASE!

YOU, MAN!

I HAVE NO SILVER, NO GOLD.

OH.

BUT WHAT I *DO* HAVE I'LL GIVE TO YOU!

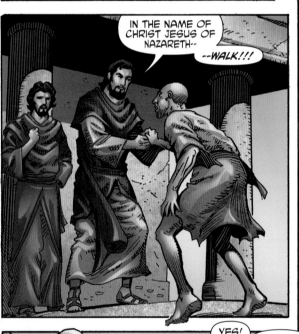

IN THE NAME OF CHRIST JESUS OF NAZARETH--

--WALK!!!

WHAT? I...I'M STANDING! MY LEGS ARE *WHOLE!*

COME, PRAY WITH US!

YES! YES! THANK YOU, GOD, FOR SENDING ME THESE MEN!

AND MORE AND MORE PEOPLE BECAME CHRIST-FOLLOWERS.

AND, LIKE HIS LORD, HE ALSO UPSET THOSE RELIGIOUS LEADERS IN CHARGE.

BY WHAT POWER--

--IN WHOSE NAME--

--HAVE YOU HEALED THAT MAN?

ARE WE ON TRIAL FOR HEALING A MAN?

WE HEALED HIM IN THE NAME OF JESUS CHRIST!

THE ONE *YOU* REJECTED!

THESE ARE JESUS-FOLLOWERS!

WHAT DO WE DO?

RUMORS OF THIS MIRACLE ARE SPREADING!

WE ORDER THEM TO NEVER SPEAK IN JESUS' NAME AGAIN!

YOU ARE FORBIDDEN TO TALK OR TEACH IN THE NAME OF JESUS!

IS IT RIGHT TO OBEY YOU OR GOD?

THERE IS ONLY ONE ANSWER TO THAT.

PETER AND JOHN WERE RELEASED WITH MORE STERN WARNINGS.

OF COURSE, THEY DID NOT HEED THOSE WARNINGS.

AND EVEN MORE PEOPLE FOLLOWED CHRIST.

PEOPLE BROUGHT THE SICK OUT TO PETER TO BE HEALED.

GOD'S POWER WAS EVEN IN PETER'S SHADOW.

AND ONCE MORE, THE HEARTS OF THE LEADERS WERE JEALOUS.

THEY HAD THE APOSTLES ARRESTED.

BUT THIS TIME, THERE WAS NO TRIAL.

INSTEAD...

COME OUT!

GO PREACH IN THE TEMPLE COURTS!

THAT MORNING...

...YOU HUNG HIM FROM A CROSS, BUT GOD RAISED HIM FROM THE DEAD!

HOW DID THEY GET OUT?

ARREST THEM!

THEY WERE FLOGGED, AND WERE ONCE MORE WARNED NOT TO PREACH ABOUT JESUS.

ONCE MORE, THEY IGNORED IT.

PETER TRAVELED TO SAMARIA AND MANY OTHER PLACES, HEALING AND LAYING HANDS ON PEOPLE.

90

IN THE TOWN OF JOPPA, HE EVEN BROUGHT A LITTLE GIRL BACK FROM DEATH.

TABITHA, ARISE.

MANY BELIEVED, BUT THEY WERE ALL JEWS.

THEN, ONE DAY ABOUT NOON PETER WAS PRAYING.

HE WAS HUNGRY, AND FOOD WAS BEING PREPARED, BUT HE FELL INTO A TRANCE.

PETER, GET UP, KILL, AND EAT.

BUT LORD, NO! I HAVE NEVER EATEN ANYTHING THAT IS UNCLEAN OR IMPURE!

WHAT GOD HAS MADE CLEAN, DO NOT CONSIDER IMPURE OR UNHOLY!

NOW, THREE MEN ARE LOOKING FOR YOU.

I SENT THEM TO YOU MYSELF. GO WITH THEM.

GREETINGS! I BELIEVE YOU ARE LOOKING FOR ME!

MY COMMANDER, CORNELIUS, PRAYS TO YOUR GOD.

AN ANGEL TOLD HIM TO SEND FOR YOU.

PLEASE, COME TO HIS HOME AND GIVE HIM A MESSAGE.

91

THE NEXT DAY, AT THE HOUSE OF CORNELIUS THE CENTURION...

THANK YOU, RABBI PETER, FOR GRACING US WITH YOUR HOLY--

CORNELIUS! STAND UP!

I AM ONLY A MAN, NOT WORTHY OF WORSHIP.

I WAS AFRAID YOU WOULD NOT COME BECAUSE I AM NOT JEWISH.

GOD HAS JUST SHOWN ME THAT I AM NOT TO CALL ANY MAN IMPURE OR UNHOLY.

WHY DID YOU CALL ME?

FOUR DAYS AGO, AN ANGEL APPEARED TO ME WHILE I PRAYED.

HE SAID, "GOD HAS HEARD YOUR PRAYERS.

"SEND FOR PETER, IN JOPPA, TO COME TO YOU."

AND SO, MY FRIENDS AND FAMILY ARE HERE!

READY TO HEAR GOD'S MESSAGE!

PETER SPOKE, TELLING THEM EVERYTHING. THE PEOPLE LISTENED.

FOR THE FIRST TIME, GENTILES WERE FILLED WITH THE HOLY SPIRIT.

RETURNING TO JERUSALEM, THE OTHER APOSTLES WERE NOT AS RECEPTIVE.

YOU ATE WITH UNCIRCUMCISED MEN?

YES! HOW CAN WE DENY THAT GOD HIMSELF LET HIS HOLY SPIRIT FALL UPON THEM?

IF GOD IS GOING TO GIVE THEM THAT GIFT--

--WHO AM I TO STAND IN HIS WAY?

IT SEEMS GOD HAS EXTENDED THE REPENTANCE THAT LEADS TO LIFE TO THE GENTILES AS WELL!

ABOUT THIS TIME, HEROD AGRIPPA BEGAN PERSECUTING THE CHRIST-FOLLOWERS.

HOPING TO MAKE THE JEWISH LEADERS HAPPY, HE ARRESTED MANY CHRISTIANS – PETER INCLUDED.

HE EVEN HAD JAMES, BROTHER OF JOHN, PUT TO DEATH.

HEROD INTENDED TO HAVE PETER EXECUTED AS WELL.

HEROD'S INTENTIONS WERE NOT GOD'S, THOUGH.

GET UP!

HURRY!

WHAT?

MUST BE ANOTHER VISION...

THEY AREN'T DOING ANYTHING, BUT THIS ISN'T A VISION, IS IT?

NO!

GOD HAS SENT YOU TO DELIVER ME! THANK YOU SO MUCH.

PETER SPREAD THE GOSPEL MAINLY TO THE JEWS.

PAUL, A NEWER CHURCH LEADER, MINISTERED MAINLY TO GENTILES.

IN ANTIOCH, THEY CAME INTO CONFLICT.

PETER! I'D LIKE A WORD WITH YOU!

WHAT'S ON YOUR MIND?

WHY HAVE YOU STOPPED EATING WITH THE GENTILE BELIEVERS?

I... I...

BECAUSE OF WHAT THE JEWISH BELIEVERS MIGHT THINK?

I KNOW MANY RESENT THAT THE GENTILE BELIEVERS DON'T FOLLOW JEWISH LAW.

BUT WE'RE FORGIVEN THROUGH CHRIST, NOT THE LAW!

HYPOCRITE! YOU WERE THE FIRST TO PREACH CHRIST TO THE GENTILES!

I... I...

YOU'RE RIGHT. WE'RE WRONG. I'LL FIX IT.

EVEN AS A CHURCH FATHER, PETER MADE MISTAKES AND ACCEPTED CORRECTION.

AFTER THIS, LITTLE IS KNOWN ABOUT PETER'S ACTIVITIES. IT IS BELIEVED THAT MARK WROTE HIS GOSPEL BASED ON PETER'S RECOLLECTIONS.

...AND HE SAID, "PEACE, BE STILL," AND THE WIND AND WAVES STOPPED...

PETER WROTE TWO LETTERS THAT WERE COLLECTED INTO THE NEW TESTAMENT.

TO GOD'S CHOSEN PEOPLE, EXILES THROUGHOUT PONTUS, GALATIA, CAPPADOCIA...

BECAUSE OF SOME DIFFERENCES IN THE WAY THE TWO LETTERS ARE WORDED--

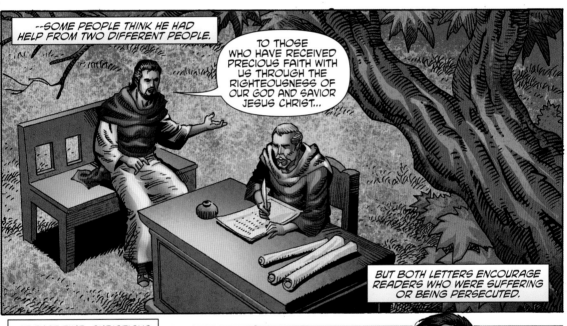

--SOME PEOPLE THINK HE HAD HELP FROM TWO DIFFERENT PEOPLE.

TO THOSE WHO HAVE RECEIVED PRECIOUS FAITH WITH US THROUGH THE RIGHTEOUSNESS OF OUR GOD AND SAVIOR JESUS CHRIST...

BUT BOTH LETTERS ENCOURAGE READERS WHO WERE SUFFERING OR BEING PERSECUTED.

AT THAT TIME, CHRISTIANS WERE BEING PERSECUTED BY GOVERNMENT AND RELIGIOUS LEADERS.

IN HIS FIRST LETTER, HE WROTE:

"...REJOICE THOUGH YOU HAVE SUFFERED GRIEF IN ALL KINDS OF TRIALS.

"...THEY PROVE THE GENUINENESS OF YOUR FAITH..."

95

AND ALSO, "DEAR FRIENDS, DO NOT BE SURPRISED AT YOUR FIERY TRIALS...

"...AS IF SOMETHING STRANGE WAS HAPPENING TO YOU...

"...BUT REJOICE BECAUSE YOU PARTICIPATE IN CHRIST'S SUFFERINGS..."

HE ENCOURAGED THEM TO NEVER GIVE UP HOPE, NO MATTER WHAT.

IN HIS SECOND LETTER, HE ALSO WANTED TO GIVE HOPE.

"...WE LOOK FORWARD TO A NEW HEAVEN AND EARTH, WHERE THERE WILL BE ONLY RIGHTEOUSNESS.

"DEAR FRIENDS, WHILE WAITING FOR THESE THINGS TO COME... LIVE LIVES THAT ARE PEACEFUL, PURE, AND BLAMELESS

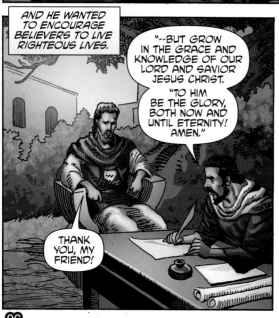

AND HE WANTED TO ENCOURAGE BELIEVERS TO LIVE RIGHTEOUS LIVES.

"--BUT GROW IN THE GRACE AND KNOWLEDGE OF OUR LORD AND SAVIOR JESUS CHRIST.

"TO HIM BE THE GLORY, BOTH NOW AND UNTIL ETERNITY! AMEN."

THANK YOU, MY FRIEND!

PAUL'S FIRST LETTER TO THE CORINTHIANS MENTIONS THAT PETER TOOK HIS WIFE ALONG FOR HIS MISSIONARY WORK.

SOME ANCIENT WRITINGS CLAIM HE WENT AS FAR AS BRITON.

MORE RELIABLE SOURCES SAY HE MAY HAVE GONE TO CORINTH OR EVEN BABYLON.

AND IT IS BELIEVED HE SPENT HIS FINAL YEARS IN ROME.

BUT ROME WAS NOT A SAFE PLACE FOR CHRISTIANS AT THAT TIME.

IT IS COMMONLY BELIEVED PETER, AND POSSIBLY HIS WIFE, WERE ARRESTED.

VICTIMS OF THE ROMAN EMPEROR NERO'S PERSECUTION OF CHRISTIANS.

HE MAY HAVE BEEN IMPRISONED AT THE MAMERTINE PRISON, ALSO KNOWN AS THE TULLIANUM.

THIS MAY BE THE SAME PLACE PAUL WAS IMPRISONED AND TORTURED BEFORE HIS DEATH.

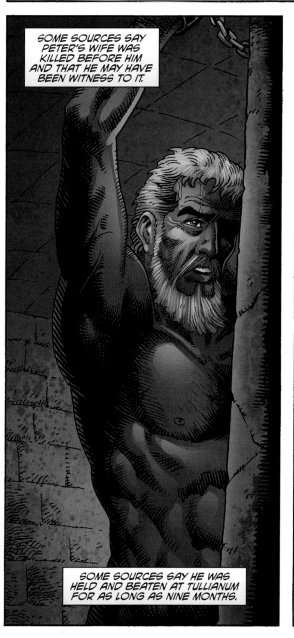

SOME SOURCES SAY PETER'S WIFE WAS KILLED BEFORE HIM AND THAT HE MAY HAVE BEEN WITNESS TO IT.

SOME SOURCES SAY HE WAS HELD AND BEATEN AT TULLIANUM FOR AS LONG AS NINE MONTHS.

EVEN IF THE EXACT DETAILS OF PETER'S DEATH ARE NOT KNOWN--

--THEY DO FIT THE ACCOUNT OF PETER'S DEATH THAT JESUS SPOKE:

"IN YOUR YOUTH, YOU DID AS YOU CHOSE.

"YOU DRESSED YOURSELF--

"--AND WENT WHERE YOU PLEASED.

YOU WISH TO BE LIKE YOUR MASTER, CHRISTIAN?

YOU WILL DIE LIKE HIM, TOO.

PLEASE--

"IN YOUR AGE--

--I AM A SINFUL MAN. PLEASE, CRUCIFY ME UPSIDE DOWN.

I AM UNWORTHY TO DIE IN THE SAME WAY AS HIM.

VERY WELL.

"YOU WILL STRETCH OUT YOUR HAND.

"OTHERS WILL DRESS YOU AND YOU WILL GO WHERE THEY TAKE YOU."

BUT EVEN IF THE EXACT DETAILS OF HIS DEATH ARE NOT KNOWN, THE IMPORTANT DETAILS OF HIS LIFE ARE.

HE LIVED AND DIED AS HE DESCRIBED HIMSELF IN HIS SECOND LETTER: "PETER, A SERVANT AND AN APOSTLE OF CHRIST JESUS."

JUDAS

Son of James, not Iscariot

"THEN JUDAS (NOT JUDAS ISCARIOT) SAID, 'BUT, LORD, WHY DO YOU INTEND TO SHOW YOURSELF TO US AND NOT TO THE WORLD?'"
JOHN 14:22 (NIV)

NAME: JUDAS, SON OF JAMES
ALSO POSSIBLY KNOWN AS:
LEBBAEUS, THADDAEUS, JUDE

FAMILY: JAMES, EITHER BROTHER OR FATHER (POSSIBLY JAMES, SON OF ZEBEDEE; IF TRUE, JOHN WOULD BE HIS UNCLE AND ZEBEDEE WOULD BE HIS GRANDFATHER)

OCCUPATION: POSSIBLY A FISHERMAN (ESPECIALLY IF HE BELONGED TO THE FAMILY OF ZEBEDEE)

HIS NAME WAS JUDAS. AN HONORABLE NAME, WHEN HE WAS GIVEN IT--

--BUT ANOTHER MAN DISHONORED IT.

BUT THEY SUGGEST MUCH ABOUT HIS CHARACTER.

SO HE WAS CALLED OTHER NAMES: JUDAS, NOT ISCARIOT; JUDE, SON OF JAMES; LEBBAEUS; AND THADDAEUS.

HIS NAMES AND ONE QUESTION THAT HE ASKED JESUS ARE ALL THAT IS KNOWN ABOUT HIM.

"JUDAS, NOT ISCARIOT": TO AVOID CONFUSION WITH JESUS' BETRAYER.

"THADDAEUS" AND "LEBBAEUS": POSSIBLE NICKNAMES OR SURNAMES.

IF THEY WERE NICKNAMES, THEY SUGGEST OTHERS THOUGHT HE WAS A KIND, GENTLE MAN.

HE WAS THERE FROM THE BEGINNING TO THE END.

"JUDE, SON OF JAMES." WAS HIS FATHER JAMES, BROTHER OF JOHN AND SON OF ZEBEDEE?

IT IS POSSIBLE.

DID HE PREFER THESE NAMES BECAUSE OF THE OTHER JUDAS?

"THADDAEUS" MEANS "DEAR," "BELOVED" OR "GIFT OF GOD."

"LEBBAEUS" MEANS "A MAN OF HEART."

HE WAS THERE IN THE UPPER ROOM, WHERE HE ASKED HIS QUESTION.

...SOON I WILL LEAVE, BUT I WILL NOT LEAVE YOU ALONE.

THE FATHER WILL GIVE YOU A COUNSELOR: THE SPIRIT OF TRUTH.

THE WORLD DOES NOT SEE OR KNOW HIM.

BUT YOU KNOW THE SPIRIT--

--BECAUSE HE IS WITH YOU AND WILL BE IN YOU.

YOU SEE, I AM IN MY FATHER, AND YOU ARE IN ME.

TO YOU WHO LOVE ME, I WILL LOVE AND REVEAL MYSELF.

AND THEN JUDAS SPOKE.

HIS ONLY RECORDED WORDS, REVEALING A TENDER, GENTLE HEART.

BUT LORD, WHY DO YOU REVEAL YOURSELF TO US ONLY?

WHY NOT TO THE WORLD?

I TEACH YOU WHILE I AM WITH YOU.

THE HOLY SPIRIT WILL BRING MY TEACHINGS BACK TO YOU.

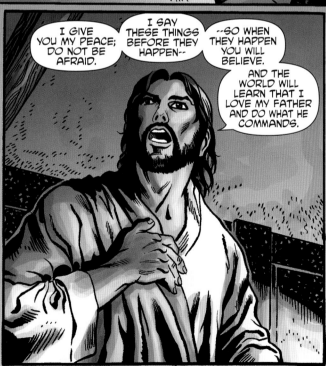

I GIVE YOU MY PEACE; DO NOT BE AFRAID.

I SAY THESE THINGS BEFORE THEY HAPPEN--

--SO WHEN THEY HAPPEN YOU WILL BELIEVE.

AND THE WORLD WILL LEARN THAT I LOVE MY FATHER AND DO WHAT HE COMMANDS.

ANDREW
"The First Disciple"

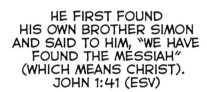

HE FIRST FOUND
HIS OWN BROTHER SIMON
AND SAID TO HIM, "WE HAVE
FOUND THE MESSIAH"
(WHICH MEANS CHRIST).
JOHN 1:41 (ESV)

NAME: ANDREW

FAMILY: PETER, HIS BROTHER;
HE LIVED WITH PETER AND
PETER'S WIFE AND MOTHER-
IN-LAW; FATHER, JOHN.

CONNECTIONS TO OTHER APOSTLES:
CLOSE FRIEND OF THE OTHER
FISHERMEN, PARTICULARLY
JAMES AND JOHN.

OCCUPATION: FISHERMAN

SIMON, I WON'T BE GOING HOME WITH YOU TODAY.

WHY NOT, BROTHER? AREN'T YOU TIRED?

I WANT TO HEAR THIS BAPTIZER FROM THE JORDAN RIVER.

THEY SAY HE SPEAKS POWERFULLY, WITH THE SPIRIT OF ELIJAH.

MANY ARE CONFESSING SINS AND BEING BAPTIZED.

HMM. LET ME KNOW WHAT YOU HEAR.

I MAY BE GONE FOR A WHILE.

WE'LL MANAGE WITHOUT YOU SOMEHOW.

OH, I'M SURE YOU WILL, BROTHER. I'LL BE BACK IN A FEW DAYS, MAYBE A WEEK.

ANDREW, LIKE MANY YOUNG JEWISH MEN OF THE TIME...

...AWAITED THE SAVIOR PROMISED BY GOD THROUGH THE PROPHETS CENTURIES AGO.

THEY AWAITED A SAVIOR WHO WOULD RESCUE THEIR PEOPLE FROM BONDAGE.

DON'T JUST REPENT.

PRODUCE THE FRUIT THAT GOES WITH TRUE REPENTANCE.

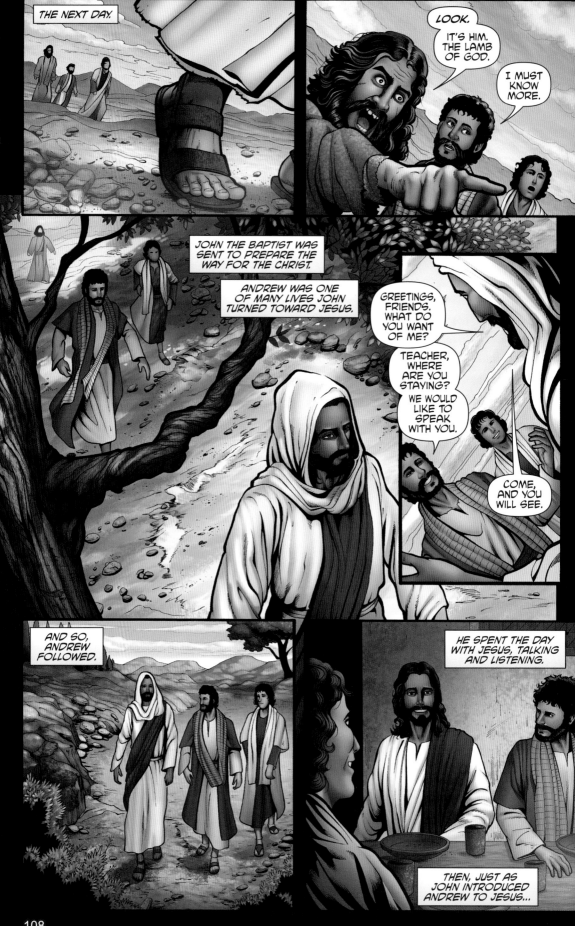

THE NEXT DAY.

LOOK. IT'S HIM. THE LAMB OF GOD.

I MUST KNOW MORE.

JOHN THE BAPTIST WAS SENT TO PREPARE THE WAY FOR THE CHRIST.

ANDREW WAS ONE OF MANY LIVES JOHN TURNED TOWARD JESUS.

GREETINGS, FRIENDS. WHAT DO YOU WANT OF ME?

TEACHER, WHERE ARE YOU STAYING? WE WOULD LIKE TO SPEAK WITH YOU.

COME, AND YOU WILL SEE.

AND SO, ANDREW FOLLOWED.

HE SPENT THE DAY WITH JESUS, TALKING AND LISTENING.

THEN, JUST AS JOHN INTRODUCED ANDREW TO JESUS...

110

WHAT DID HE SAY?

THAT'D COST NEARLY A YEAR'S WAGES!

HE TOLD US TO GIVE THE PEOPLE SOMETHING TO EAT.

I KNOW. HE WANTS US TO GIVE THE FOOD WE HAVE TO THE PEOPLE.

COME WITH ME, BOY.

SURE!

WHAT ARE YOU DOING?

GIVING HIM WHAT WE HAVE.

HERE IS WHAT WE HAVE, JESUS.

THIS BOY HAS FIVE LOAVES OF BARLEY BREAD AND TWO FISH.

BUT HOW FAR CAN THAT GO WITH SUCH A CROWD?

HAVE THE PEOPLE SIT DOWN.

115

SO MANY TEACHINGS.

ON SOME OCCASIONS, ANDREW WAS PART OF A SMALLER, SPECIAL GROUP.

LOOK AT THOSE MAGNIFICENT BUILDINGS.

AND YET EVERY ONE OF THOSE STONES WILL BE THROWN DOWN.

NOT ONE WILL BE LEFT ON ANOTHER.

WHEN WILL THAT HAPPEN?

AND BY WHAT SIGN CAN WE KNOW YOUR WORDS ARE ABOUT TO TAKE PLACE?

IT IS GOOD TO ASK ME THAT.

YOU SHOULD WATCH SO YOU ARE NOT DECEIVED.

MANY WILL COME IN MY NAME AND SAY THEY ARE THE CHRIST.

THEY WILL SAY THE TIME IS NEAR.

BE ON YOUR GUARD. YOU WILL BE GIVEN OVER TO THE CITY COUNCILS AND FLOGGED IN SYNAGOGUES.

OTHER TIMES, THE SMALL GROUP WAS ONLY THREE--

JAMES, JOHN, AND ANDREW'S BROTHER, SIMON PETER.

THESE THREE HAD WITNESSED THE TRANSFIGURATION.

THEY HAD BEEN IN THE ROOM WHEN JESUS RAISED JAIRUS'S DAUGHTER FROM THE DEAD.

JESUS CALLED THE SAME THREE TO WAIT WITH HIM WHILE HE PRAYED...

...IN THE GARDEN OF GETHSEMANE.

SIT HERE WHILE I GO OVER THERE AND PRAY! PETER, JAMES, JOHN...

...JOIN ME, PLEASE.

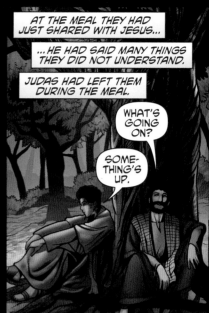

AT THE MEAL THEY HAD JUST SHARED WITH JESUS...

...HE HAD SAID MANY THINGS THEY DID NOT UNDERSTAND.

JUDAS HAD LEFT THEM DURING THE MEAL.

WHAT'S GOING ON?

SOME-THING'S UP.

JESUS PRAYED.

THE APOSTLES SLEPT.

UNTIL...

GET UP! MY BETRAYER IS COMING.

JESUS OF NAZARETH?

I AM HE.

117

AFTER JESUS' ARREST...

...THE APOSTLES FLED.

THE APOSTLES WENT INTO HIDING.

IT'S JOHN!

LET HIM IN.

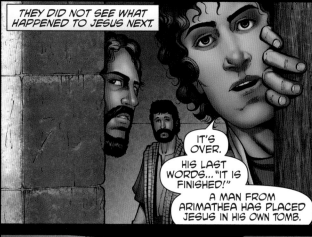

THEY DID NOT SEE WHAT HAPPENED TO JESUS NEXT.

IT'S OVER.

HIS LAST WORDS... "IT IS FINISHED!"

A MAN FROM ARIMATHEA HAS PLACED JESUS IN HIS OWN TOMB.

THEY WAITED...

...IN FEAR...

...IN MOURNING...

...IN HOPE- LESSNESS.

UNTIL...

IT'S EMPTY!

JESUS' TOMB IS EMPTY!

COME SEE!

CAN IT BE?

LATER, AFTER PETER AND JOHN HAD INVESTIGATED...

IT'S EMPTY, JUST AS MARY SAID.

EXCEPT FOR HIS BURIAL LINEN.

MY FRIENDS!

HAVE NO FEAR.

PEACE BE WITH YOU.

IT'S TRUE. IT'S HIM.

JESUS SPENT MORE TIME WITH THEM AFTER HE RETURNED.

HE EXPLAINED WHAT HAD HAPPENED AND WHY.

I HAVE FULFILLED THE SCRIPTURES THAT SAID THE MESSIAH MUST SUFFER, DIE, AND RISE FROM THE DEAD ON THE THIRD DAY...

...AND THAT IN HIS NAME—IN MY NAME—REPENTANCE AND FORGIVENESS WILL BE PREACHED TO ALL NATIONS.

JESUS ASCENDED INTO HEAVEN.

HIS NAME WAS ANDREW.

LIKE MANY YOUNG JEWISH MEN OF THE TIME...

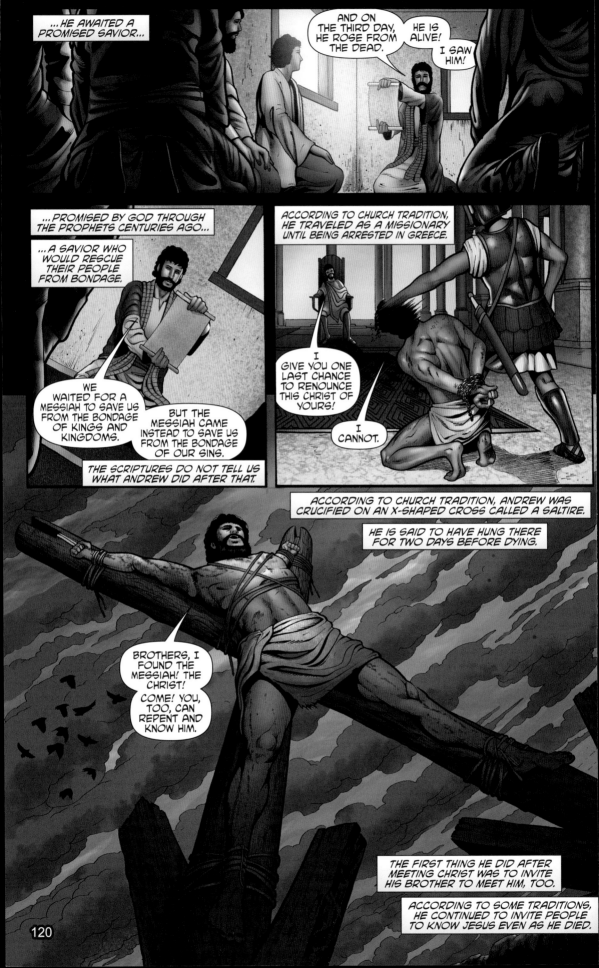

...HE AWAITED A PROMISED SAVIOR...

AND ON THE THIRD DAY, HE ROSE FROM THE DEAD.

HE IS ALIVE!

I SAW HIM!

...PROMISED BY GOD THROUGH THE PROPHETS CENTURIES AGO...

...A SAVIOR WHO WOULD RESCUE THEIR PEOPLE FROM BONDAGE.

WE WAITED FOR A MESSIAH TO SAVE US FROM THE BONDAGE OF KINGS AND KINGDOMS.

BUT THE MESSIAH CAME INSTEAD TO SAVE US FROM THE BONDAGE OF OUR SINS.

THE SCRIPTURES DO NOT TELL US WHAT ANDREW DID AFTER THAT.

ACCORDING TO CHURCH TRADITION, HE TRAVELED AS A MISSIONARY UNTIL BEING ARRESTED IN GREECE.

I GIVE YOU ONE LAST CHANCE TO RENOUNCE THIS CHRIST OF YOURS!

I CANNOT.

ACCORDING TO CHURCH TRADITION, ANDREW WAS CRUCIFIED ON AN X-SHAPED CROSS CALLED A SALTIRE.

HE IS SAID TO HAVE HUNG THERE FOR TWO DAYS BEFORE DYING.

BROTHERS, I FOUND THE MESSIAH! THE CHRIST!

COME! YOU, TOO, CAN REPENT AND KNOW HIM.

THE FIRST THING HE DID AFTER MEETING CHRIST WAS TO INVITE HIS BROTHER TO MEET HIM, TOO.

ACCORDING TO SOME TRADITIONS, HE CONTINUED TO INVITE PEOPLE TO KNOW JESUS EVEN AS HE DIED.

120

BARTHOLOMEW, also known as NATHANAEL

"The Son of Israel"

WHEN JESUS SAW NATHANAEL APPROACHING, HE SAID OF HIM, "HERE TRULY IS AN ISRAELITE IN WHOM THERE IS NO DECEIT." JOHN 1:47 (NIV)

NAME: BARTHOLOMEW
ALSO KNOWN AS: NATHANAEL

FAMILY: BARTHOLOMEW MEANS "SON OF TOLMAI,"
SO IT IS LIKELY HIS FATHER WAS NAMED TOLMAI

CONNECTIONS TO OTHER APOSTLES:
CLOSE FRIEND OF PHILIP

OCCUPATION: FISHERMAN

IN PROVERBS, THE TEACHER SAYS, "AS IRON SHARPENS IRON, SO ONE MAN SHARPENS ANOTHER."

THIS DESCRIBES THE FRIENDSHIP OF PHILIP AND NATHANAEL.

...AND JOHN – THE BAPTIZER, NOT JAMES'S BROTHER – TOLD THEM, "I AM THE ONE CALLING IN THE DESERT:

"'MAKE STRAIGHT THE WAY OF THE LORD!'"

LIKE THE PROPHET ISAIAH SAID!

EXACTLY, NATHANAEL!

JOHN SPEAKS SO FORCEFULLY, SO TRUTHFULLY.

THEY SAY HE SPEAKS WITH THE SPIRIT OF ELIJAH!

GOD SPEAKS THROUGH HIM IN WAYS I HAVE NEVER SEEN BEFORE.

BUT HE SAID HE IS NOT THE CHRIST.

YES, HE KEEPS SAYING THAT THERE IS ONE TO COME AFTER HIM.

AFTER SO LONG, COULD THE MESSIAH COME IN OUR GENERATION?

IF JOHN TRULY SPEAKS OF THE CHRIST, THE MESSIAH, HE'S PROBABLY ALREADY HERE!

WE JUST HAVE YET TO SEE HIM!

SEE YOU TOMORROW, NATHANAEL!

TOMORROW, PHILIP!

COULD WE GET TO SEE THE MESSIAH?

NATHANAEL AND PHILIP (AND POSSIBLY SOME OF THE OTHER FISHERMEN) DISCUSSED THE SCRIPTURES TOGETHER.

TOGETHER, THEY EXPLORED THE LAW AND THE PROPHETS.

TOGETHER, THEY GREW SPIRITUALLY, SEEKING GOD AND GOD'S TRUTH...

...AND WAITING FOR THE MESSIAH PROMISED TO THEM IN THE SCRIPTURES.

NATHANAEL!

IT'S HIM!

IT'S HIM!

WE'VE FOUND HIM!

THE ONE MOSES WROTE ABOUT!

THE ONE THE PROPHETS WROTE ABOUT!

JESUS, SON OF JOSEPH, OF NAZARETH!

NAZARETH? THAT PLACE? CAN ANYTHING GOOD COME FROM THERE?

IT'S A NASTY PLACE WITH ONLY TWO TYPES OF PEOPLE: BAD AND WORSE!

JUST COME AND SEE FOR YOURSELF!

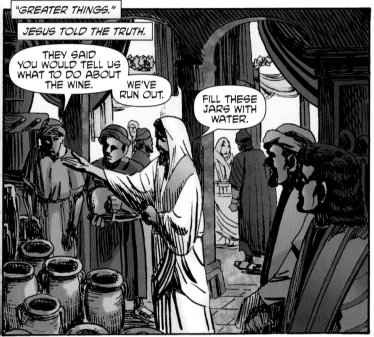

"GREATER THINGS."

JESUS TOLD THE TRUTH.

THEY SAW MANY MIRACLES, FROM JESUS' FIRST...

... TO HIS MANY HEALINGS...

...TO HIS GREATEST MIRACLE...

...THE MIRACLE OF HIS MISSION HERE ON EARTH...

...TO HIS FINAL MIRACLE, ASCENDING INTO HEAVEN...

GO, AND MAKE DISCIPLES OF ALL NATIONS.

...AFTER WHICH, JUST AS HE SAID...

...THEY SAW GOD'S ANGELS.

WHY ARE YOU LOOKING IN THE SKY?

HE WILL RETURN THE SAME WAY YOU SAW HIM GO INTO HEAVEN.

NATHANAEL FOLLOWED JESUS' COMMANDS.

I STUDIED THE SCRIPTURES AND WITNESSED THE ANCIENT WORDS OF THE PROPHETS COME TO LIFE...

...IN JESUS, WHO WAS CRUCIFIED!

IT IS BELIEVED HE WENT TO INDIA...

...WHERE HE WAS BEATEN AND CRUCIFIED FOR PREACHING JESUS AS MESSIAH FOR ALL MEN.

LIKE MANY OTHERS, HE SEEMS TO HAVE DIED ON A CROSS, JUST LIKE JESUS...

...BEFORE BEING REUNITED WITH HIS MESSIAH.

PHILIP

"The Hellenistic Jew"

PHILIP SAID, "LORD, SHOW
US THE FATHER AND THAT
WILL BE ENOUGH FOR US."
JOHN 14:8 (NIV)

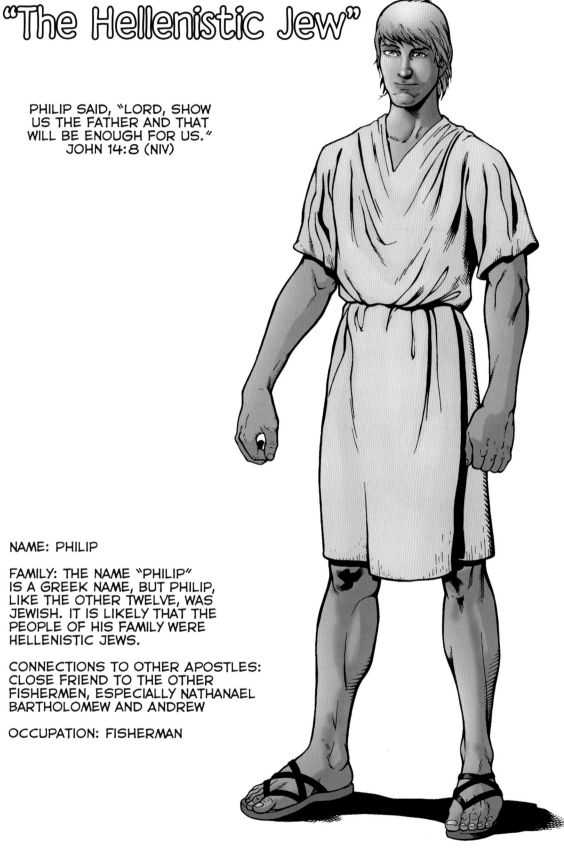

NAME: PHILIP

FAMILY: THE NAME "PHILIP"
IS A GREEK NAME, BUT PHILIP,
LIKE THE OTHER TWELVE, WAS
JEWISH. IT IS LIKELY THAT THE
PEOPLE OF HIS FAMILY WERE
HELLENISTIC JEWS.

CONNECTIONS TO OTHER APOSTLES:
CLOSE FRIEND TO THE OTHER
FISHERMEN, ESPECIALLY NATHANAEL
BARTHOLOMEW AND ANDREW

OCCUPATION: FISHERMAN

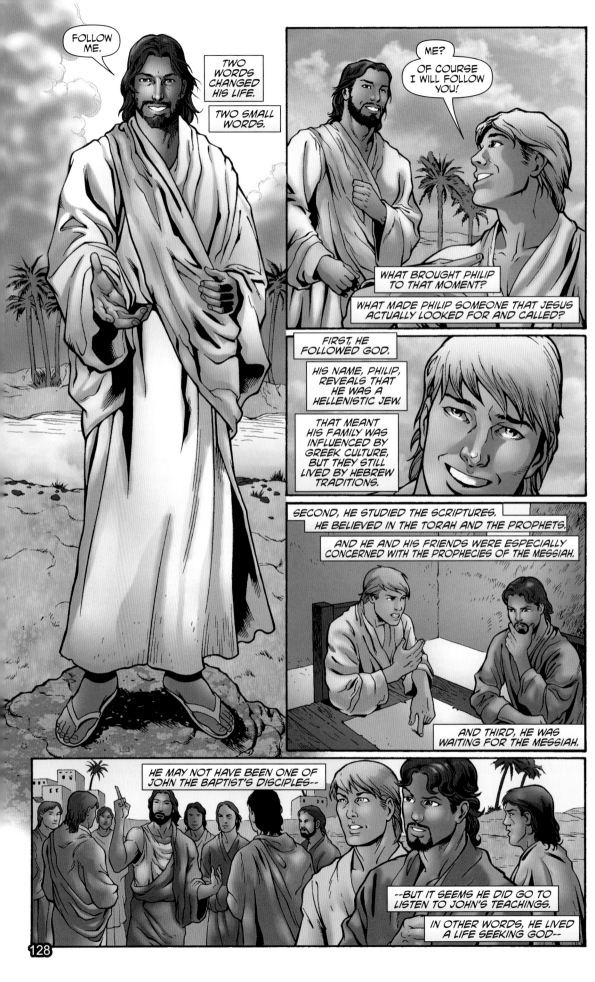

--AND GOD FOUND HIM.

OF COURSE I WILL FOLLOW YOU, BUT I HAVE A FRIEND!

HE HAS BEEN WAITING FOR YOU, JUST LIKE ME!

LET ME GO GET HIM!

OF COURSE.

THE FIRST THING PHILIP DID AFTER GETTING THE INVITATION TO FOLLOW JESUS--

NATHANAEL! WE HAVE FOUND HIM!

THE ONE MOSES WROTE ABOUT!

THE ONE THE PROPHETS WROTE ABOUT!

THE MESSIAH!

--WAS TO FIND HIS FRIEND NATHANAEL AND INVITE HIM TO FOLLOW JESUS, TOO!

TWO WORDS -- "FOLLOW ME" -- AND PHILIP'S LIFE WAS CHANGED.

FOREVER.

TWO WORDS -- "FOLLOW ME" -- AND PHILIP WAS INVITED TO SEE THE WORLD CHANGE.

FOREVER.

THE WAIT WAS OVER, BUT PHILIP STILL HAD MANY LESSONS TO LEARN ABOUT FOLLOWING CHRIST.

HE WAS THERE WHEN JESUS WAS TEACHING THE 5,000 PEOPLE IN THE WILDERNESS.

5,000 PEOPLE WHO DID NOT EXPECT TO BE THERE SO LONG, AND WHO WERE GETTING HUNGRY.

WE SHOULD SEND THE PEOPLE HOME, JESUS.

THEY ARE HUNGRY.

SO FEED THEM.

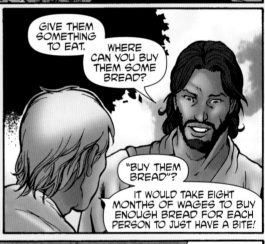

GIVE THEM SOMETHING TO EAT.

WHERE CAN YOU BUY THEM SOME BREAD?

"BUY THEM BREAD"? IT WOULD TAKE EIGHT MONTHS OF WAGES TO BUY ENOUGH BREAD FOR EACH PERSON TO JUST HAVE A BITE!

SO WHAT DO WE HAVE THAT WE CAN GIVE THEM?

THIS BOY HAS FIVE SMALL LOAVES OF BREAD AND TWO SMALL FISH.

THAT WON'T DO MUCH WITH SO MANY.

GIVE IT TO ME AND HAVE EVERY-ONE SIT DOWN.

JESUS THANKED GOD FOR THE BREAD, THEN BROKE THE BREAD--

--GIVING IT TO THE DISCIPLES TO GIVE TO THE PEOPLE.

TWELVE BASKETS OF BREAD WERE LEFT OVER. ONE BASKET FOR EACH OF THE TWELVE DISCIPLES.

PHILIP LEARNED ABOUT GOD'S PROVISION THAT DAY.

THIS IS WHY I AM HERE, BUT MY SPIRIT IS DISTRESSED! WHAT DO I SAY? "FATHER, SAVE ME FROM THIS HOUR"? NO, INSTEAD I SAY, "FATHER, GLORIFY YOUR NAME!"

I HAVE GLORIFIED IT.

AND I WILL GLORIFY IT AGAIN.

WAS THAT THUNDER?

NO, AN ANGEL!

THE VOICE YOU HEARD WAS FOR YOUR BENEFIT, NOT MINE.

JUDGMENT IS COMING, AND THE RULER OF THIS WORLD WILL BE CAST AWAY.

BUT WHEN I AM LIFTED UP FROM THE EARTH, I WILL GATHER ALL MEN TO ME.

PUT YOUR TRUST IN THE LIGHT, WHILE YOU STILL HAVE IT.

WALK IN THE LIGHT BEFORE DARKNESS COMES, SO YOU MAY BE SONS OF LIGHT.

NO ONE UNDERSTOOD THEN THAT JESUS SPOKE OF HIS COMING DEATH.

NOR DID THEY UNDERSTAND THAT HE CAME NOT JUST AS THE JEWISH PEOPLE'S MESSIAH, BUT THE MESSIAH FOR ALL MEN.

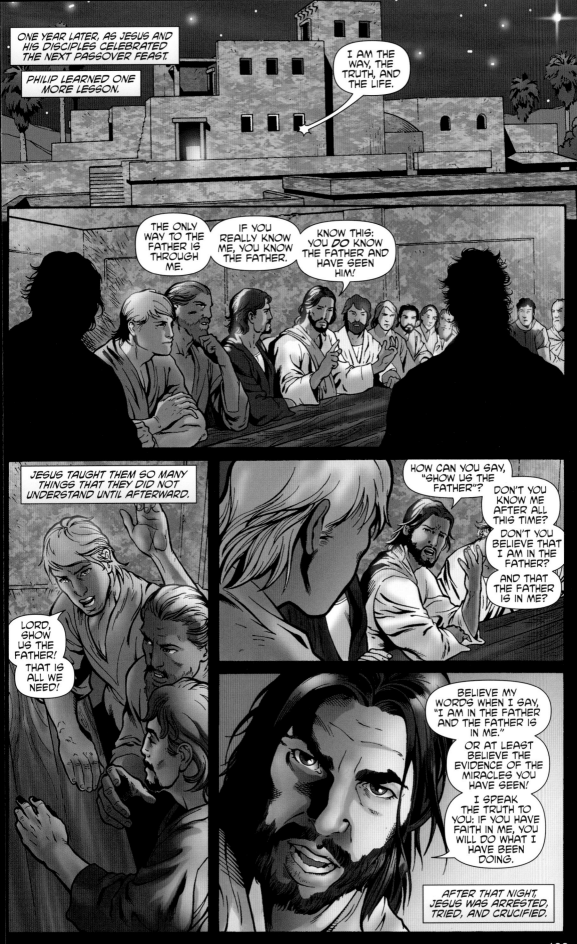

JESUS WAS LIFTED FROM THE EARTH, AS HE SAID.

AFTER HIS RESURRECTION AND BEFORE HE LEFT THE EARTH, THE DISCIPLES BEGAN TO UNDERSTAND.

FOR PHILIP, THOSE TWO WORDS NEVER LOST THEIR POWER.

TRADITION SAYS HE WENT AS FAR AS UPPER ASIA, TEACHING JESUS' GOSPEL.

THE FIRST THING PHILIP DID AFTER JESUS SAID "FOLLOW ME" WAS TO INVITE HIS FRIEND, TOO.

AND AFTER JESUS ROSE INTO HEAVEN, PHILIP CONTINUED INVITING PEOPLE TO FOLLOW.

IT IS THOUGHT HE DIED IN HELIOPOLIS.

TRADITIONS SAY HE WAS PUT IN PRISON, SCOURGED, AND EVENTUALLY CRUCIFIED OR STONED.

LIKE A WHEAT KERNEL, PHILIP DIED.

BUT MANY SEEDS HAD LIFE BECAUSE HE INVITED THEM TO COME TO CHRIST.

ALL BECAUSE OF THOSE TWO WORDS: "FOLLOW ME."

JAMES
"Son of Thunder"

JESUS ANSWERED,
"YOU DO NOT KNOW
WHAT YOU ARE ASKING.
ARE YOU ABLE TO DRINK
THE CUP THAT I AM TO
DRINK?" THEY SAID
TO HIM, "WE ARE ABLE."
MATTHEW 20:22 (ESV)

NAME: JAMES, SOMETIMES
CALLED JAMES THE GREAT
OR JAMES THE ELDER

FAMILY: OLDER BROTHER OF
JOHN; SON OF ZEBEDEE;
POSSIBLY THE FATHER OF
JUDAS, KNOWN AS THADDAEUS

OCCUPATION: FISHERMAN

WHENEVER THE BIBLE LISTS THE TWELVE, JAMES IS NAMED EITHER SECOND OR THIRD.

JESUS CALLED JAMES AND HIS YOUNGER BROTHER, JOHN, TO LEAVE THEIR FISHING BUSINESS AND...

COME WITH ME!

JAMES AND JOHN WERE NOT JUST PART OF THE TWELVE.

ALONG WITH PETER, THEY WERE PART OF JESUS' INNER CIRCLE.

THOSE THREE WITNESSED JESUS BRINGING JAIRUS'S DAUGHTER BACK TO LIFE.

I TELL YOU TO GET UP, LITTLE GIRL.

THEY WERE PRESENT WHEN JESUS WAS TRANSFIGURED...

...AND THEY SAW JESUS SPEAK TO ELIJAH AND MOSES.

THE THREE RECEIVED SPECIAL TEACHING FROM JESUS.

JESUS ASKED THE THREE TO COME WITH HIM TO PRAY...

...BEFORE HE WAS ARRESTED IN THE GARDEN OF GETHSEMANE.

IT WAS NOT THEIR FINEST HOUR.

BUT VERY LITTLE IS SAID ABOUT JAMES.

JAMES AND HIS BROTHER, JOHN, HAD A NICKNAME--

"THE SONS OF THUNDER."

AND LONG BEFORE THAT NIGHT IN THE GARDEN AND THE TERRIBLE EVENTS THAT FOLLOWED...

...THEY SHOWED THEY DESERVED IT.

BAD NEWS, JESUS.

THE VILLAGE AHEAD HAD ROOM FOR US...

UNTIL THEY HEARD WE WERE TRAVELING TO JERUSALEM.

I KNEW WE SHOULD HAVE AVOIDED SAMARIA.

THIS IS NOT RIGHT!

JERUSALEM IS WHERE THE TEMPLE IS.

THEY KNOW PASSOVER IS COMING.

SINCE THE TIME OF ELIJAH, THIS REGION HAS BEEN FULL OF HEATHENS...

...IDOLATERS AND PAGANS!

JESUS, DO YOU WANT US TO CALL DOWN FIRE ON THAT VILLAGE...

...AS ELIJAH DID WHEN AHAZIAH'S MEN CONFRONTED HIM?

DO YOU EVEN KNOW WHAT KIND OF SPIRIT YOU SPEAK WITH? THE SON OF MAN DID NOT COME TO DESTROY MEN'S LIVES. THE SON OF MAN CAME TO SAVE THEM.

WE WILL GO TO THE NEXT VILLAGE AND INQUIRE THERE.

JAMES AND JOHN KNEW JESUS WAS SPECIAL...

...BUT THEY STILL DID NOT FULLY UNDERSTAND WHY...

...EVEN WHEN JESUS EXPLAINED IT CLEARLY.

CLEARLY THEY DID NOT UNDERSTAND WHAT JESUS WAS SAYING.

CONSIDER WHAT HAPPENED SOON AFTER.

IN JERUSALEM, THE SON OF MAN WILL BE BETRAYED INTO THE HANDS OF THE PRIESTS. HE WILL BE CONDEMNED, SCORNED, BEATEN, AND CRUCIFIED.

ON THE THIRD DAY, HE WILL RISE.

JAMES AND JOHN'S MOTHER, ALSO A FOLLOWER OF JESUS, APPROACHED JESUS.

JESUS, I WOULD ASK A FAVOR.

WHAT WOULD YOU ASK OF ME?

LET ONE OF MY SONS SIT AT YOUR RIGHT HAND IN YOUR KINGDOM.

AND LET THE OTHER SIT AT YOUR LEFT HAND IN YOUR GLORY.

YOU DO NOT KNOW WHAT YOU ASK.

CAN YOU DRINK FROM THE CUP I MUST DRINK?

CAN YOU BE BAPTIZED WITH THE BAPTISM I AM BAPTIZED WITH?

WE CAN!

YOU WILL, INDEED. YOU WILL DRINK FROM MY CUP. YOU WILL BE BAPTIZED WITH MY BAPTISM.

BUT AS FOR YOUR QUESTION, TO SIT AT MY RIGHT OR LEFT HAND?

THAT IS NOT MINE TO GRANT.

MY FATHER HAS PREPARED THOSE PLACES.

AND THOSE PLACES BELONG TO THE ONES HE PREPARED THEM FOR.

CAN YOU BELIEVE THEM?

TRYING TO BE FIRST IN THE KINGDOM AGAIN...

COME HERE, MY FRIENDS. ALL OF YOU.

ONCE AGAIN, JESUS TAUGHT THE TWELVE.

BUT THEY DID NOT FULLY UNDERSTAND UNTIL LATER.

THE KINGS OF THE GENTILES HAVE POWER AND AUTHORITY, AND THEY USE IT. THEY LORD IT OVER EVERYONE. IT SHOULD NOT BE SO WITH YOU. INSTEAD...

"WHOEVER WANTS TO BE GREAT AMONG YOU...

"...MUST BE A SERVANT.

"WHOEVER WANTS TO BE FIRST...

"...MUST BE THE SLAVE TO ALL.

139

"FOR EVEN THE SON OF MAN DID NOT COME TO BE SERVED...

"...BUT TO SERVE..."

...AND TO GIVE HIS LIFE AS A RANSOM FOR MANY.

WHEN JESUS DIED, JAMES SAW WHAT IT MEANT TO DRINK FROM THAT CUP.

BUT THIS "SON OF THUNDER" DID NOT QUIETLY DISAPPEAR.

HE PREACHED JESUS' MESSAGE LOUDLY.

HEROD AGRIPPA DID NOT LIKE THIS.

HE PERSECUTED THE FOLLOWERS OF CHRIST.

WE ARREST YOU IN HEROD THE KING'S NAME!

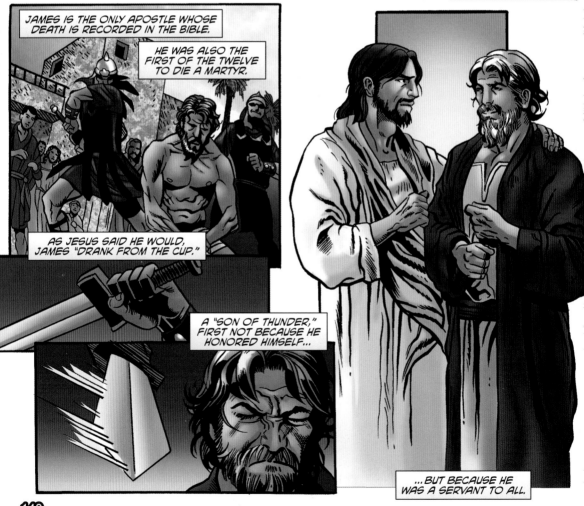

JAMES IS THE ONLY APOSTLE WHOSE DEATH IS RECORDED IN THE BIBLE.

HE WAS ALSO THE FIRST OF THE TWELVE TO DIE A MARTYR.

AS JESUS SAID HE WOULD, JAMES "DRANK FROM THE CUP."

A "SON OF THUNDER," FIRST NOT BECAUSE HE HONORED HIMSELF...

...BUT BECAUSE HE WAS A SERVANT TO ALL.

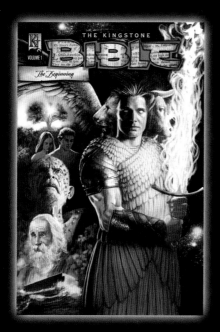

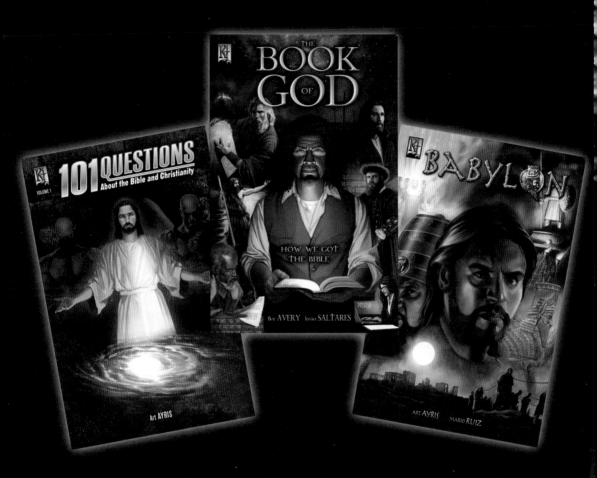